THE Q4 QUEST
for Financial Advisors

*The secret of how top performers are
developing tomorrow's best practice today!*

CHRIS CAHILL
AND
TREVOR BONNELL

authorHOUSE®

AuthorHouse™
1663 Liberty Drive
Bloomington, IN 47403
www.authorhouse.com
Phone: 833-262-8899

© 2020 Chris Cahill and Trevor Bonnell. All rights reserved.

No part of this book may be reproduced, stored in a retrieval system, or transmitted by any means without the written permission of the author.

Published by AuthorHouse 08/11/2020

ISBN: 978-1-7283-6910-5 (sc)
ISBN: 978-1-7283-6973-0 (e)

Library of Congress Control Number: 2020914613

Print information available on the last page.

Any people depicted in stock imagery provided by Getty Images are models, and such images are being used for illustrative purposes only.
Certain stock imagery © Getty Images.

This book is printed on acid-free paper.

Because of the dynamic nature of the Internet, any web addresses or links contained in this book may have changed since publication and may no longer be valid. The views expressed in this work are solely those of the author and do not necessarily reflect the views of the publisher, and the publisher hereby disclaims any responsibility for them.

CONTENTS

Preface ix
Introduction xi
    Exercise: Preliminary Profile xv

SECTION 1

Q1 – Motivation 1
    Motivation 1 - Passion 2
    Motivation 2 - People 7
        Exercise: Who Matters Most 10
    Motivation 3 - Purpose 12
        Exercise: Personal Vision Statement 13
        Exercise: Personal Mission Statement 15

Q2 – Reservations 16
    Reservations 1 – Pain 19
        Exercise: Reservations and Pain 23
    Reservations 2 – Partiality 24
        Exercise: Partiality Reservations 26
    Reservations 3 – Pride 27
        Exercise: Pride Reservations 33

Q3 – Situation 35
    Situation 1 - Passions 36
        Exercise: Passion Assessment 37
    Situation 2 - Personality 38
        Exercise: Personality Type 39
        Exercise: FBGM Aptitude 43
    Situation 3 - Personal Stories 43
        Exercise: Personal Past – Part A 45
        Exercise: Present Story – Part B (Be Magnetic) 46

Situation 4 - Professional Resources 47
    Exercise: Resources – Time 49
    Exercise: Resources – Money 51
    Exercise: Resources – Relationships 55

Q4 – Expectation **57**
Precision 57
    Exercise: The Three Eulogies 60
Pairing 62
    Exercise: Self, Service, Or Stuff 63
Prioritization 64
    Exercise: Horizon (Or Look Back Test) Test 68
    Exercise: Quick Litmus Test/Reverse Check-Up 72

SECTION 2: EXERCISES

Introduction 77
    Exercise: Preliminary Profile 80

Q1 – Motivation **83**
    Exercise: Fear and Desire 83
    Exercise: Who Matters Most 87
    Exercise: Personal Vision Statement 91
    Exercise: Personal Mission Statement 94

Q2 – Reservations **100**
    Exercise: Pain 100
    Exercise: Partiality 103
    Exercise: Pride Reservations 106
    Exercise: Get It Out of Your Head 108
    Exercise: Quick Litmus Test/Reverse Check-Up 112

Q3 – Situation **114**
    Exercise: Passion Assessment 115
    Exercise: FBGM Aptitude and Personality Type 117
    Exercise: Personal Past - Part A 124
    Exercise: Present Story – Part B (Be Magnetic) 126

Exercise: Resources – Time... 129
Exercise: Resources – Money 132
Exercise: Resources – Relationships 136
Exercise: Relationships 137
Exercise: Quick Litmus Test/Reverse Check-Up 142

Q4 – Expectation **143**
Exercise: The Three Eulogies 143
Exercise: Self, Service, Or Stuff.. 147
Exercise: Priority Path 149
Exercise: Quick Litmus Test/Reverse Check-Up 155

Special Thanks 157
Works Cited.. 159
Testimonies 161

PREFACE

Book – Workbook – Interactive Experience

Top performers can be found in all walks of life and in every career. These all-stars make winning look easy and living life look fun. They play everything to win and frankly usually do. It's as if they have some allusive secret for success, or a mysterious set of rules only they know, while everyone else fights for every inch. The truth is, there is a secret, and we call it Q4 (mainly because that is how it was passed on to us). Now, this book, *The Q4 Quest*, and its supplemental workbook will guide you on your Quest to find the secret for yourself.

Q4's wisdom is not just something to read about. It is something you must experience. That is why this is more than just a book and a workbook. Through the use of technology, you can now immerse yourself in the full Quest experience. Follow along online as you build your profile and develop your character. Like playing an adventure video game, you can 'level-up' and uncover new opportunities. The difference is you are the real-life avatar, and the game is life. When you win online, you will find you are also winning in real life.

Start your Quest today and transform your daily life into a true adventure. Through the parables of Papa Joe, an unlikely hero and biker-slash-sage-business consultant, authors Chris Cahill and Trevor Bonnell unveil timeless wisdom and nearly twenty years of success testimonies. Coupled with your personal workbook and interactive online experience, you will have the benefits of psychology, science, and sales all woven together into a four-part journey that will transform your businesses and your life forever.

INTRODUCTION

Setting the stage

"Every day, we have a choice. Do we go left, right, or simply tread water?"

Creating a system to maximize fulfilment, minimize pain, bring clarity to the choices you make, and create an environment rich with positive reinforcement is the goal of this book and the Quest!

Everyone deserves a chance to fulfill their potential. Everyone should be shown the secret.

> *Consider this: "Even the lack of a decision is a decision, and therein lies the challenge," I can still hear Trevor say now. Trevor is often looking for ways to "nerd" things up with his science. As one of the two authors whose voices will be heard throughout this book, he brings the science of success to our story while Chris reveals the "art" of success through an idealized caricature he calls Papa Joe. Papa speaks in the present tense while Trevor's voice often reveals lessons learned in the past through his personal Q4 Quest.*
>
> *Today, Trevor graciously reminds everyone to, "not fall short of their potential simply because we have not taken the time to understand how we make smarter decisions." That is what drives us both to share this Quest with everyone so passionately.*

This book is a fresh start for anyone who might be burned-out and stuck, or just hungry for more. *The Q4 Quest* is more than just another self-help book, even though it will help you tremendously. *The Q4 Quest* will forever change the way you see and think about your situation. You will make wiser decisions than ever before and subsequently witness business and life transforming before you. From determining where you want to eat dinner to launching a new business, getting married, or building your career, Q4 will improve your situation. The challenge is that the secret of Q4 cannot be taught; it must be found.

This is where *The Q4 Quest* comes in. If Q4 can be compared to the "Holy Grail," then *The Q4 Quest* is the map to find it. Specifically, *The Q4 Quest* becomes your four-part framework for first discovering your innermost motivations and reservations and then ultimately develop your situation, and ideal expectations. You will find that unlike so many self-help books, *The Q4 Quest* is far less about telling you what to do and all about telling you how you can "do you."

Once you see Q4, you will wonder as others have, "Why haven't I done this sooner, and why hasn't everyone figured this out?"

To open your eyes to *The Quest for Q4*, meet Papa Joe. Joe will guide you and our characters through parables and true testimonies throughout the four sections of your quest. Along the way, you have time to apply Q4's transformational exercises to your own life.

The first part of the book is the narrative itself. An actual journey with Ron and his teacher, slash guide, Papa Joe. Each section of the journey will build on the previous section, and each section concludes with introspection and a call to action.

The second half of the book is your Quest. It reads like a companion workbook. By supplementing the story with completing your own exercise you are sure to have and informational and a transformational experience. You may further augment your emersion into The Q4 Quest online by building your own profile and receiving resources and support for further coaching and accountability.

Now, let the Quest begin.

The Diner

Ron was sitting at the diner, pondering his next move in the puzzle we call life when, like a tornado, the front doors to the diner opened and Papa Joe walked in. He looked more like the front cover subject of a Harley Davidson magazine than a consultant. He wore a leather vest, scruffy beard, combat boots, and he even had a chain wallet.

With a firm but jovial voice that the whole place could hear, Joe yelled to his old friend, "Hey, Ron, how are you, my brother?"

Ron looked up from his booth. He was startled but excited to see his old friend. Grinning like a child, he said, "So good to see you, Joe," as he stood from his seat for a hug.

Joe reciprocated with a manly bear hug, nearly lifting his friend off the ground. "You too, Ron, you too."

"So, how's it going?" Joe asked, sliding into the booth across from his old friend.

"Well, you know, same old stuff," Ron said. He had asked for the meeting but clearly wasn't ready to get into the weeds.

He elected for his trained "I'm fine" speech coupled with a well-rehearsed smile, but Joe wouldn't have it. He stared him down like a schoolyard principal waiting for a more honest answer.

"Let me try that again. Ron, how are you REALLY doing, my brother?"

Ron dove in, and once he did, it just kept flowing. The simple truth was Ron was not fine, and Joe knew it. Ron was a middle-aged small business owner cracking under the pressures of surmounting bills. He was overwhelmed by a digital world running faster than he could; he was disappointed by how distant he had gotten with his family, particularly his daughter; and he knew his house was out of order, let alone his future finances.

"Thank you, Ron. I appreciate your honesty and trusting me with that confidence. It sounds like I am right on time, and I am guessing by your story you aren't familiar with Q4, are you?"

"I don't think so. What's Q4?" Ron asked.

"Well, Q4, my friend, is a way of life for people looking to break free and break through to new potential."

"Slow down, Joe, that sounds like corny self-help stuff to me."

"Maybe, but let me ask, do you need help?" Joe asked, pausing to let the truth of his sarcasm sink in.

"I am not sure, to be honest. Maybe I just need an ear to listen."

"Fair enough. As you know, I am a consultant, but please remember I am also here first as a friend and a person who cares. At the end of the day, if working together doesn't excite you, then I'll love you where you're at, and simply enjoy the coffee and the company before moving on."

"I appreciate that, Joe. I really do. So, go on, tell me more about the Q4 thing."

Papa Joe slid his coffee cup over, making room to write on a napkin. He pulled a pen out from his leather vest pocket, clearing his throat, and said, "Q4, my friend, is where we are going together. I will show you a new way of making decisions that, if you embrace, will change the way you see everything. It will make your bright brighter and your whites whiter, and new opportunities will present themselves everywhere."

Eager and curious, Ron stared at Joe. "Go on!"

"Now, think about this," said Joe. "According to a study published by the Oxford University Press in 2013, the average adult makes about 35,000 choices each day, and most of these take place with no conscious knowledge. In fact, we make nearly 300 decisions a day on food alone!

"These choices run subconsciously; more like the operating system of our phones or computers. You don't have to think about your next breath, and throughout the day, you don't think about the habits you've built up over a lifetime.

"Now, think of your habits like operating systems. How many old phones or computers do you have that are bogged down, or flat broke because they became cluttered and overburdened with junk? Your habits are built up around you the same way. When there is a surplus of poor habits in place, it's easy to become encumbered quickly. The Q4 Quest begins by uncovering and reprogramming your sub-conscience with your true inner motivations so you can begin to purge your operating system of all the other junk."

"Makes sense, Joe, please keep going."

"Well, when our brain has been cluttered and bogged down with all the bad information and propaganda of our media-laden society, what do you think happens?" asked Joe.

This time Ron appeared to feel relieved his problems were not entirely his fault.

"You got it?" Joe smiled as he drew a compass on his napkin. "The Q4 Quest comprises four elements that will create your code, or framework if you will, to help you make great decisions not only for yourself and for today, but also for everyone you care about, and for life."

Hesitant, yet eager to learn more, Ron probed again. "What are these four mysterious elements you've got? Let's hear 'em, Joe."

"I am glad you asked." Joe pointed back to the napkin where he drew kind of an x shape to make four quadrants. He wrote a word in each:

    I.   MOTIVATIONS
    II. RESERVATIONS
    III. SITUATION
    IV. EXPECTATION

"That's it?" questioned a disappointed looking Ron.

"That's it," Joe said. "It's not complicated, but it's not easy either. Trust me on that, but here is what I need you to keep in mind. I am not here to merely help you build a formal improvement plan, and I am not simply going to dole out some life rules or professional suggestions for changing something about how you do some part of your life."

"Then what do you intend to do?" Ron quipped.

"Well, it's like this. If you give a man a fish, you feed him for a day, but if you teach him to fish, you feed him for life, right?"

"Yeah, sure."

"So, think of Q4 as learning how to fish with your mind. I believe in time you will appreciate the benefit of learning to 'be' far more than being told what to 'do.'"

"Okay, hippie," Ron smiled, "so what am I fishing for?"

Joe lit up. "I love that question, Ron. Let's find out!"

Exercise: Preliminary Profile

This Quest is complete with transformational exercises and our interactive Q4 Quest Online.

The first step of the Quest begins here with a foundational or preliminary profile. While this step may be simple, do not use that as a reason to skip ahead. Each step builds on the last, and often the mysteries are missed without context. This is your life, and you owe it to yourself to play to win.

Preliminary Profile – (Visit the back of the book)

For your full experience, visit the interactive Q4 Quest Online, where your Quest comes to life.

SECTION 1

Q1

MOTIVATION

The 3Ps of Motivation:

- **Passion – The dichotomy of your fear and desires**
  Exercise: Fear and Desire
- **People – Because your "who" is your "why"**
  Exercise: Who Matters Most?
  Exercise: Relationship Mapping
- **Purpose – Plotting Your Quest**
  Exercise: Personal Vision Statement
  Exercise: Personal Mission Statement

Your True Motivation

As Joe has done with others so many times before, he began Ron's journey, and ours, not with a focus on where we were going but why we felt compelled to go there.

"Inner peace, harmony, and ultimately one's success is driven most by 'why' something is done, not 'how' or 'what,'" Papa Joe said to Ron.

Your motivations may also be the most misunderstood and underappreciated factor in any improvement process. So, why is that, and what can you do to fix it?

> *Consider this: When digging to uncover what your true motivation is, understand that multiple theories exist. They*

are all founded in science. All of them may be useful at some point. This book blends the ideas of the three theories below.

- *Maslow's hierarchy of needs - Maslow's theory relates to fear and desire by both pointing one up the pyramid, or hierarchy of human needs. Fulfilling needs based on biological principles helps you attain the highest level of achievement in your life.*

- *Vroom's theory of expectancy - In this model, the participant expects to minimize pain (fear) and maximize pleasure (desire) in the choices they make.*

- *Behaviorism - This model explains motivation in terms of reinforcement schedules paired with antecedents and consequences.*

"Step one," said Joe, "is to get a clear understanding of your motivations. Specifically, the 'what' and 'who' a person cares most about." (But not necessarily in that order as we will explore later).

So, getting back to Ron, let us look a bit closer at this two-sided coin by examining the dichotomy of fear and desire.

Ron initially seemed a bit uneasy opening up about those topics. After all, he wanted solutions, not psychology, and very few people take the time to get to the heart of a matter like Papa Joe. In fact, society has left most of us uncomfortable with sharing this level of introspection with someone else. Fortunately, Ron was serious about wanting help, and he trusted Joe, so we can dive in deep.

Motivation 1 - Passion

Fear and desire

Sensing Ron's unease, Joe took the time to clarify further what he meant by exploring the dichotomy of fear and desire.

"What is motivation, really?" asked Joe rhetorically. "Motivation is a driver—the reason why we do what we do! Motivation may be either seen or unseen, and it may come from variables outside of ourselves, or it may be a fire deep within us. At the core, motivation may be understood as the manifestation of our more deep-seated fears and desire," Joe continued.

"We may desire a healthy marriage, a new home, or maybe a promotion or simply to support a meaningful cause. We may fear being lonely, poor, misunderstood, or sick. But here's the thing. They are really two sides of the same coin. A desire to travel may be stated as a fear of not seeing the world. A desire to be a good provider may be described as the fear of losing financial stability. Even a desire to experience the abundance of life may be expressed as a fear of poor health or even death. So, we start by focusing on the carrot and not the stick.

Drawn in by the conversation, Ron said, "A friend of mine says it this way: 'Anxiety [or fear] is imagination wasted.'"

"Exactly. Pause and let that sink in. Now, we could also say that another way: 'fear is desire unrealized,' and inversely 'desire is fear conquered.' Let's consider that for a minute. Simply put, fear is demoralizing while desire inspires, so we can focus our energy on the fear or the desire, and your choice can make all the difference."

> *Consider this: In 2016, a study by The London School of Economics and Political Science determined that relationships, not income, are among the top factors which prove to be the root of happiness. Another study conducted at Harvard over 80 years ago determined that it's mostly having "good friends [that] protects people from mental and physical decline, and [even] gives a better idea of how long someone's life will be than their social class, IQ or [even] genes."*
>
> *When we look back on our lives from the threshold, I am certain we will all wish we had spent more time with the people, and activities, that we truly care about, not less. Doing so with intentionality is joy, sustainable significance, and that is living a life inspired.*
>
> *Joy is something more than the happiness that comes and goes like the weather. Joy is the healthy and intentional pursuit*

of happiness while happiness is more determined by our surroundings. Happiness can come and go like the weather while joy transcends mere experience finding contentment with the good, and bad, of our journey.

As an athlete endures intense training, the Q4 Quest motivates us through any pain and loss that will inevitably come with knowing and loving others. As Alfred Lord Tennyson wrote, "Tis better to have loved and lost than to have never loved at all."

Exercise: Fear and Desire

Consider the following exercise, using the picture as a guide. With a whiteboard or sheet of paper, draw a line down the center creating two halves. For your convenience, this exercise is also in the back of the book.

On the left side, write the title 'Fear,' and on the right side, write 'Desire.' Begin by thinking about your fears and write down the top one or two. Then ask yourself, "If this were to occur, what is the worst that could happen?" and write it down.

Repeat: what else, what else, what else . . . until you have identified the absolute worst thing that could happen in your mind or exhausted your possibilities. It usually takes a half a dozen or so scary layers to exhaust our fears well.

Now, using the 'Desires' column, work directly across from each previous fear. Write what you desire to happen instead of the originally described fear. By the time you get to the bottom (including each fear/desire), you will have painted an accurate picture of what truly matters to you.

To further develop your relationship mapping, visit the workbook section of this Quest, and update your profile online.

Internal Motivators

Shift focus from Fear . . . → **To Desire**

Shift focus from Fear . . .	To Desire
- Not planning well enough for my future	- Clarity and Confidence
- Losing financial security	- Peace of mind / financial security
- Losing home or lifestyle	- Comfortably providing for family
- Unstable family / shame / risk	- Making memories with loved ones
- Loss of hope	- Love, joy, and peace

(Observe any items that include other people, even if it is only your own family. It is also other people that can determine how you view these motivators.

So, now what?

No Fear!

After the pause to fears and desires, Joe continued, "Remember, these are both drivers towards the same goals. Negative reinforcement works as compliance like the seatbelt light in your car."

"People don't like that" Ron said.

"Exactly!" Joe jumped in. "The only way to get the red light to turn off is by buckling your seat belt. Most people consider buckling your seat belt a good behavior. Let's relate this to the exercise now. Losing financial security is a fear (negative reinforcement): a fear that can drive you to make better financial behavior choices."

Joe warned Ron that compliance only helps you reach the bare minimum of your goal. Set this goal carefully if fear is the best tool for the behavior. Your minimum has to be well defined and high. Also, your negative reinforcement must be strong for it to work. For example, we will look back at the seat belt goal later. The goal is to insert the buckle into the clasp. The only way to get the dangerous tattletale red light to turn off is to follow through with the goal. People do not like to be uncomfortable (seatbelt) until the current situation (warning light and bell) is more annoying the change itself. The same is true when we need to make changes in how we conduct business or manage our lives.

Finding Desire

Replacing Fear with Desire is what behaviorists call positive reinforcement, and it works!

Joe explained this concept to Ron, "This is easier for most people to understand because you are adding something good, not taking something away. If you want your kid to clean their dishes, offer them candy to do a good job."

"Adding the candy is a good reason for them to do it even when they don't want to, because who wants to do the dishes?" chuckled Ron.

"Right again!"

From a practical point of view, no one wants to buy insurance, but most people want to make sure that they can provide for and protect their families should the unexpected happen. Focusing on the family is far more likely to motivate while focusing on medical needs, and the cost of insurance is likely to promote positive steps taken.

Looking back at your whiteboard or the sheet of paper you wrote on previously, continue filling out your fears and desires, this time with a stronger focus on additional desires. Remember to consider the people in your life like the previous example and to restate all fears as positive motivators.

> *Consider this: Studying the field of behavioral psychology, Trevor recollected the Skinner theory of operant conditioning. The point at which positive reinforcement involves the addition of a reinforcing stimulus following behavior makes it more likely the behavior will occur again in the future. When a favorable outcome, event, or reward occurs after an action, it will strengthen a particular response or behavior.*
>
> *Switching fear to desire allows you to introduce more positive reinforcement outcomes to your path. This also increases the likelihood of you attaining the goal of your Q4 quest.*

Motivation 2 - People

From "WHAT" to "WHO."

Joe knew he had captured Ron's attention and worked to sink in the proverbial hook.

"We have said that motivators might be external or internal, so let us start by looking at some key external motivators. Besides the obvious health and safety concerns, the top three things that most people worry about include money, job security, and relationships. Considering that the underlying worry with job security still boils down to money, we might say that there are just two broad categories: money (stuff) and relationships (service)."

These two world views generally divide all mankind. We either belong to the majority faction: those who are driven mostly by the desire to acquire, or the second smaller group, which seeks first to serve and help others. In other words, our motivations, while they may be as unique as we are, ultimately can be traced back to either stuff or service.

Recognize now that stuff, or money itself, is not bad. In fact, it is essential. Ask any church or non-profit, and they will surely concur, "no money = no mission." However, when the love of money or material gain becomes more important than the love for others, we are surely heading for a fall. We ought to ask ourselves this fundamental question, "Do I use people to improve my resources and financial situation, or do I use my resources and financial situation to further the lives of other people?" Would others say the same thing?

Unfortunately, the world around us rewards materialism. Politicians get elected, wars get waged, companies grow, and economic markets advance. The idealist inversely goes unsung in small country churches, back alley soup kitchens, and nondescript dinner tables across the lands. It is so rare for kindness to be rewarded tangibly that when it is we make award-winning movies like *Wonder*, *Gandhi*, *Patch Adams*, *The Blind Side*, and *Hotel Rwanda* to memorialize the occasion.

Even in financial planning, which presumably is about money, the true steward recognizes that investing is far less about chasing returns and far more about providing and protecting our lifestyle for those we care most about.

Statements and charts can't capture the joy of funding a decade of retirement travel with a spouse, paying for children's schooling, donating to a favorite cause, or helping a family member launch a dream business. Yet how often do we begin by assessing our resources rather than our relationships? After all, what do we really have if we have no one to share it with?

The Lost Monk

"Consider this story of a novice monk struggling to grow closer to God," started Joe.

"After months of seeking spiritual growth with little avail, he decided to venture into the woods to be alone and to pray harder than ever before. After some time, it grew dark, and the monk looking around realized that he was now lost.

"The minutes turned into hours and eventually even days, as he wandered through the wilderness looking for a way out. Despite his prayer and best efforts, things looked more and more hopeless, and he continued to walk and pray to be saved. That's when he saw another man approaching in the distance.

"'Hooray,' he thought, 'God has answered my prayers, and I am saved.' As the man approached, the monk said to the man, 'My brother, what a blessing it is to see you. I have spent so long lost in the wilderness. Please tell me how to get home!'

"The other man replied, 'Brother, I do not know the way out either. I have also been wondering about these woods for days, praying for a sign or way out.'

"After a moment to think over the new situation, the young monk gave the man a hug and said, 'Praise God, both of our prayers have been answered.'

"'How's that?' the man asked.

'We will be alright; we have each other!'"

Called for Community

Joe leaned back signifying a change in pace and said "I have never asked anyone to paint me the picture of a perfect world and had them describe a life alone. Why? Because Our 'What' Begins with Our 'Who.'"

> *Consider this: Catching up on some articles written about connection, Trevor found one that described perfectly how our "why" or "what" is essential to our "who." Personal connection is hard-wired in the brain. When we connect with people, it releases oxytocin in the brain. Oxytocin can be described as the relationship drug of the brain. Connecting is so deeply ingrained in our biology that the body has a chemical dedicated to building relationships.*
>
> *If you have ever watched a game of football, or another sport, you will quickly see that if someone makes a touchdown or good play, they instinctively look around to give hugs and high-fives. We instinctively know that we are all made for fellowship. In all the years I have spent counseling, I (Chris) have never asked anyone to paint for me the picture of a perfect world and had them describe a life alone. Whether we are lost in the woods, or we are hoping to share in a victory, we are relational creatures and always have been. Any effort done solely in a vacuum, or solely for the benefit of the vacuum, is done in vain. Even introverts work on projects that impact or influence others and are similarly impacted and influenced by others along the way. Like the two men lost in the wilderness, we find our inner peace, personal strength, and hope through each other.*

So, if we know that anything in life worth doing is worth more when it's shared, we can see that "what" matters most to us is really a question of "who" matters most to us, and what do we do with them. Are we motivated by a desire to acquire or are we motivated by a desire to love and serve others? Are you moving along the Q4 Quest?

Exercise: Who Matters Most

This next exercise is a two-part process. Using the following chart, prime your brain for the upcoming relationship mapping exercise. Laid out below are the six tiers of our personal relationships. Now, think about how each one affects your story. Proceed to part two when you're ready, and for further development visit the workbook section of this Quest and update your profile online.

(1) Six-tier relationship model:
  1. Family – Family members and possibly their significant relations (parents, spouses, in-laws, children, grandchildren, nieces, nephews, etc.).
  2. Friends and extended Circle of Influence – close friends, neighbors, and others of personal significance such as business partners or key employees that are like family.
  3. Those you serve – Those who you are uniquely qualified and compelled to serve in business and life, such as clients, community causes, or social and political agendas.
  4. Those you serve with – Meaningful peers or colleagues such as business relationships, partners, key advisors, coaches, or family members.
  5. Champions – Key mentors and outspoken advocates who might be instrumental in your life and/or mission.
  6. Challengers – Difficult (business or personal) relationships that may prevent happiness or growth in any area.

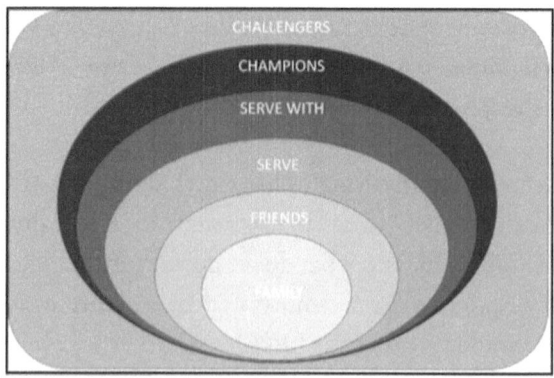

(2) Relationship Mapping

Next, expand on the previous list using the relationship mapping model depicted below.

Using a bulletin board, whiteboard, or legal pad like in this example, map your previously listed relationships and any pertinent details. (Of all the tools I have ever seen, the most effective for purposeful planning by far is "relationship mapping").

Relationship mapping helps to first visualize each of your previously collected relationships in terms of proximity and impact. Second, it makes it easy to see where decisions made might influence (or be influenced by) the people around us.

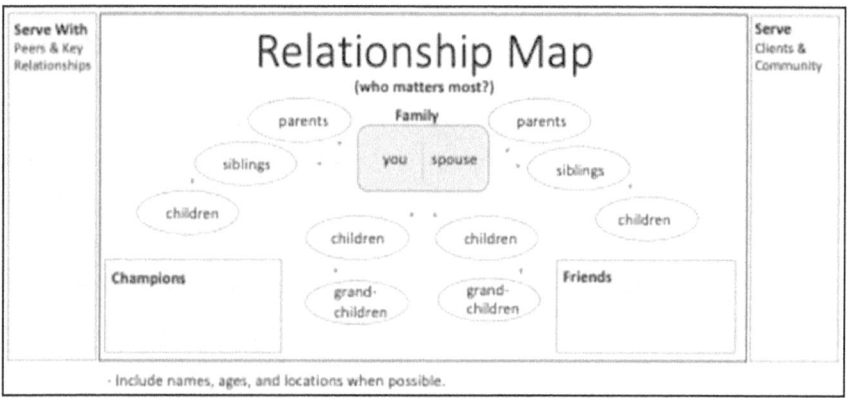

Additional Provoking Question(s): Try to answer before reading on.

- If you could design the perfect dinner with anyone living today, who would it be and why? (Was it your spouse or family member? What does your answer tell you about yourself?)
- If there's someone in your life you must interact with, but they also rub you up the wrong way, how do you deal with the situation and why? (Does your solution seek improvement by attempting to change someone else or by changing something about yourself? What does your answer tell you about yourself?)

To further develop your relationship mapping, visit the workbook section of this Quest, and update your profile online.

Motivation 3 - Purpose

Plotting Your Quest

"Stay with me, Ron!" Joe exclaimed while drawing out what would later become a 'Relationship map' for Ron. "Now that we have looked at our motivators externally, let's turn our focus inward."

Motivation is just as much about dedication because no one is excited about anything all the time, but true motivation is about being grateful for the opportunity. Through the ups and downs, what things consistently make you wake up most mornings excited to hit the ground running?

Joe continued to explain what they were digging for. He asked, "What gives you goosebumps when you think about doing it, Ron? Outside of vacation days or lazy weekends of rest, what activities happen in your daily life that make you say, 'Wow! Pinch me! I get to do this every day,' even when it's hard?

"Let's focus in on those activities, and the good news here is that, there will inevitably be less time for the activities we care little for," he continued.

To better understand what these ideal activities look like, let's look more closely at your personal vision and mission statements. Do you have them? How do they line up?

Personal Vision Statement

Helping Ron with his own vision statement, Joe asked him to close his eyes for a moment.

You should try it too. (Okay, I guess I should say read this first and then try closing your eyes).

"Now," Joe added, "with your eyes closed, visualize yourself as an instrument that has been perfectly placed, injected into this world at a precise place and time for one primary purpose—to make the world a better place. What does that look like, and what might your role be? How is the world better off because of you? This is where your personal vision statement should begin."

Unfortunately, if you have ever attended a business or leadership workshop, you have likely been instructed any number of ways to articulate that vision statement. I do not believe there is only one right way to write a vision statement, but in my humble opinion, there is a wrong way.

I don't believe it should ever be a general description of how you or your company aims to "do a good job at a fair price." A sustainably significant vision statement is bigger than that. If done with sincere thought and introspection, a vision statement is personal, inspiring, and will likely never change even when your situation or job does. A personal vision statement could be something you could literally tattoo on your arm knowing, confidently, it will accompany you anywhere in life. I know because I have done it many times.

For a timeless example of a phenomenal personal vision statement, consider Dr. Martin Luther King's vision from his "I have a dream" speech. Most of us remember how passionately he fought for equal rights, but his personal vision was even more powerful than that. His personal vision statement was to make the world a better place for all people by inspiring humanity to align itself, and its laws, with heavens and the divine.

In other words, to build a world where all people treat each other with the same respect and dignity as they would each want to be treated. Now, that's a reason to get out of bed every morning—that's a vision.

"That was his dream. What is yours, Ron?" Joe asked.

Exercise: Personal Vision Statement

> Take a moment to write down your personal vision statement.

Did you capture:

- *Your dream* – Capture how you see your life's work impacting the world or the community (like the Dr. Martin Luther King "I have a dream" vision statement).

- *Your part* – To help transition to your mission statement, capture in your journal what contribution your gifts add to that vision.
- *Your tagline* (bumper sticker) – To help make it memorable, capture in your journal your life's bumper sticker that reflects the essence of your vision.

For further development, visit the workbook section of this Quest and update your profile online.

Personal Mission Statement

Let's now learn what we can from how Joe broke down his personal mission statement. After all, for every vision there must be a mission because a dream without a plan is just wishful thinking. A mission statement essentially bridges the "who" and the "why" of our motivation to our "what" and the "how" of our expectation. At the same time, a mission statement is still much more than just our day-to-day activity.

Consider Kellogg's mission: "To nourish families so they can flourish and thrive."

Notice they did not say, "We help hungry people by making bran cereal at a competitive price."

That would be a job description, not a mission statement. Again, the focus is on relationship. Yet, think about how many mission statements you have heard or read that get this wrong and miss the mojo!

Now, consider your own mission. Do you have one? If so, does yours capture your true essence? Does your mission statement inspire you? Does it inspire others?

We could stop and spend years, maybe a lifetime right here. As our actions and our identity become increasingly consistent, an amazing thing happens; like a moth to a flame, you become a light and a beacon attracting the right relationships to your life and your business.

Exercise: Personal Mission Statement

> Take a moment to write down your personal mission statement.

Did you capture:

- Who are you compelled to serve? Write a sentence or two about who you feel you are best equipped to serve, and how?
- What are you gifted or called to do?
- How, or in what way, do you help others?

For further development, visit the workbook section of this Quest and update your profile online.

Final thoughts

"All right Joe I think I'm starting to get it. Q4 has something to do with the people in our lives?"

"That's a big part of it Ron. Q4 begins with focusing on who matters most in our hearts. It's about selflessness and in that sense it is about relationships. There is no better way to build a business or a life than with love, and there is no better way to love and be loved than to give your life to the service of others."

Q2

RESERVATIONS

The 3Ps of Our Reservations

- **Pain (of change)**
  Exercise: Pain Reservations
- **Partiality (and bias)**
  Exercise: Partiality Reservations
- **Pride (and ego)**
  Exercise: Pride Reservations

Mother Theresa summed up life when she said, "Love until it hurts and love some more . . . It's that simple." But simple can be so hard to do! So is change. The desire to change is simple. Lasting change is hard, but it does not have to be. It can be as simple as changing our minds. In other words, personal integrity. Being honest with ourselves about what 'we' want not what we do to please or impress others. Inner peace really only requires us to be honest with ourselves about what truly motivates 'us.' It requires a clear picture of who you are, what you care about, and a clearly aligned personal vision and mission.

But here's the thing. Being honest takes looking in the mirror at our own baggage, blind spots, and bias. We all have personal reservations. We carry these reservations of bias into every decision we make whether we are aware of it or not. The first step to lasting change in life is changing your mind to confront these reservations head-on.

So, to move ahead, recognize that these reservations have been instilled in most of us through not only experience but also education and training.

We must rewrite the script and let go of the lies we hold so dear if we want something more than we have today. After all, what we are doing now is getting us what we have now, but you know you have more potential in the tank.

Back to The Diner

Heading back to the diner with Ron and Papa Joe, let's look at step two of the Q4 Quest: an honest assessment of your reservations.

"Okay, Joe," Ron said irritably, "this is great and all, but we've done a lot of talking about mission statements and family trees, but I have real issues, business problems, and serious financial worries TODAY that we need to talk about."

Joe replied, "I understand, Ron, but if you want a different situation you need to do things a bit differently. Right?"

"Perhaps, but despite my current weariness, Joe, I have done alright for myself. I probably make more money than you, no offense, and frankly, I don't want to disrupt the applecart by changing the way I do things. I just want your perspective on ways I might work through my current worries and prepare for the future."

Hearing that his troubled friend still didn't get it, Joe gave him a warm smile and turned his head like a confused dog asking, "Let me get this right, you want some things to change without making any material changes?"

"I know, I know," Ron acknowledged before sipping his coffee. "I have some issues to work on, but we don't need to make more out of all this than it is. Maybe I am just tired and need a vacation."

"Know this, Ron. You're not alone. Sure, we can change anytime we want. But that assumes that we actually want to. The reality is that people don't like to change, even when we know they should. Grumpy people will usually die grumpy, and anxious people will stay anxious. Introverts will generally keep to themselves, and extroverts can't hold their tongue for too long even if they want to.

"Just look at New Year's resolutions. A recent report showed only eight percent of all New Year's resolutions are ever followed through, and most are discarded within two weeks. From weight loss to financial planning to strategic business decisions, most of us have been wired to maintain the status quo, even when it is killing us.

"Over time, we even learn to become complacent about our situation or shortcomings and lose the fire inside. We begin to die from the inside out. Therefore, typical self-help techniques and flavor-of-the year fads for finding some secret to success seldom bring anyone sustainable achievement.

"The problem is not that we need more products or services to help us change; the problem is we need to change the way we think and make decisions. By approaching change as the pain that it is, we can see similarities with how we cope by looking again to science—specifically, the grief cycle."

> *Consider this: The Grief Cycle - Kubler-Ross' research produced a grief cycle for mental health purposes that illustrates the sincere grief that comes from making changes in our lives.*
>
> *1. The phase of Pain – This phase is usually paired with the realization of change. If you ever looked in the mirror and saw a zit, then you might say, "Whoa! Something is wrong!"*
>   *a. Dealing with initial Shock*
>   *b. Denial and Avoidance*
>
> *2. The phase of Partiality – When the initial shock has worn off and the prefrontal cortex takes back over, people begin trying to understand the first phase. Based on their pre-programmed systems, they begin to analyze the shock and denial.*
>   *a. Accepting or Rejecting (confirmation bias)*
>   *b. Anger, Frustration or Depression*
>
> *3. The phase of Pride – If someone makes it through the scheme trap, then they are set up for another pitfall where*

they know something is wrong. They may seek change or help, but fail to follow through and end up in a loop of despair.
   a. Desire Change
   b. Seeking Help

4. Final phase of Acceptance and Progress. The situation can finally be accepted for what it is. The quester understands the available paths and choses can take action once again to determine where their story will go.

These phases are different for everyone. Little change or big change can amplify any of these steps. Be mindful of where you are in this process and give yourself the bandwidth to cope.

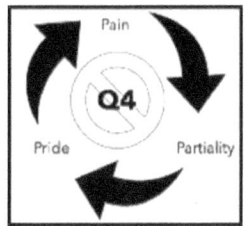

Reservations 1 – Pain

Pain of Change

Pain is temporary, yet as Julius Caesar said, "It is easier to find men who will volunteer to die than to find those who are willing to endure pain with patience." Now, without wasting space on self-help hype and motivational pep talks, let us get real. From life-planning to living out life, pain is part of the equation both physically and mentally. To paraphrase the great business mind Jim Rohm, "We must all suffer from one of two pains: the pain of discipline or the pain of regret," and the pain of regret weighs far more than the pain of discipline. With over six billion people on a spinning trampoline in space, pain is inevitable, and in life you're either in the storm or about to be as they say. We are all either running from something or running to something. We are either in the storm or we are about to be. Accepting that is the first step to rising above it.

Thinking we can talk about passion or purpose without addressing pain is both unrealistic and dangerous. Avoiding it only makes it worse and harder to cope with. For some, it's the reason we want to change. For many, it's the reason we will not. So, let's start with the problem of pain. What it is, what causes it, and what should we do with it?

In short, pain is the disparity, or the gap, between what is and what we think ought to be. A finger perhaps that should be intact but instead is missing a piece due to an accident or losing a loved one before their natural time. Emotional pain comes when the way we are feeling contrasts with our sincere desires or when the way others see us is different to the way we see ourselves. We often bring pain upon ourselves when the decisions we make or avoid making introduce inconsistencies between the roads we choose and the life we were made for.

Look at your own life. Perhaps there are traumatic events in the past where things happened that are still causing you pain? Or if others caused you pain, forgiveness may still be necessary to work through them (for your sake, not theirs). If your pain came from happenstance, it might be eased through hope for a better future. If your own choices led to your pain, self-forgiveness and hope are both in order as well as the faith or belief you are bigger than your pain and so much more than your past mistakes.

However, through the Q4 Quest, we learn to accept pain and gain the necessary clarity to further mitigate it, prepare for it, and rise above it. As Dean Koontz wrote in *Velocity*, "Pain can be endured and defeated only if it is embraced. Denied or feared, it grows." Our Quest is about accepting the pain of where we are and managing the pain of where we are going.

Without clarity about ourselves and conviction in ourselves, the disparity between who we are and who we have the potential to be increases. Just like standing with one foot on the dock and one foot on a departing boat, eventually you will either get ripped in half or fall in, and it hurts. We've all been hurt. From relationships to careers to grand dreams and expectations, everyone has setbacks and disappointments. Few pains, however, hurt more than the weight of a life lived in quiet desperation, invisibly screaming, unrecognized and alone, longing for greater impact and to live the life we know we were made for. We must bridge the gap between what is and what we feel ought to be!

So, how do we change? In a way, we don't . . . and shouldn't try! The world around us may change, but people seldom do, at least not in our "flavor." Sure, we have discussed how by doing what we've always done, we'll get what we've already got. We also understand that with a fast-paced world, whatever we've done to get where we are today will usually not get us where we want to be in the future! From the fall of ancient empires to the demise of corporate leaders like GM and Kodak, history has proven that ceasing to adapt will eventually destroy us. This is true in civilization, in business, and in life itself. After all, the only constant in life is change itself, coupled of course with how much we love to resist it.

Now, if we know we need change to grow, why do we fight so hard not to? Frankly, we don't always want to change; more often, we just wish we did. We want to be better or different or more confident, but the pain of addressing change is perceivably higher than the discomfort of today. Often our pride gets us talking about changing or taking a more noble course. It may even sound so good we convince ourselves. After all, who doesn't like the idea of improving our lives? However, the reality is until the pain of our current situation becomes greater than the perceived pain of change, most of us cannot follow through with tangible adjustment.

Denial

"Let me tell you a story," said Papa Joe as he leaned in, excited to have the stage again.

"Almost twenty years ago, a young scientist I worked with, we'll call him Ben, discovered some groundbreaking research that led to the improvement of nearly a million lives through science. Ben's discovery naturally launched an international company that provided well for his family and sent his children to top schools. Ben's research is still used for changing lives in the field today.

"Like many pioneers, Ben's initial run of success was hard to replicate, and years of similar work invested kept leading to dead ends. That's true, and in time the world caught up to Ben. Ben's company was no longer producing the income or new ideas that he once enjoyed. Ben even hired three different consultants and continued to look for ways to repackage his initial achievements with only minimal success. The reality is the world around Ben had changed, but he was not able to.

"What had made Ben so good initially was that he was not in it for the money. He wanted to find a way to make the world a better place. If he was honest, he was also fueled by his disdain for the old paradigms, which he believed led to the problems in the world he was working on. Ben was a natural-born disruptor, and his passion was just as much about the mission as it was about fighting the status quo.

"As irony would have it, his fire inside made him a success, and that very success over time made him the very person and paradigm he once thrived on fighting. He had become the paradigm and the people he needed to rely on to purchase from his company, were the very people he built his life around fighting. Ironically, he still fights today because it's who he is, but his fighting only makes him his own biggest obstruction. We are all blind at times, and our egos overshadow our altruism, but how can we honestly approach the world if we can't honestly approach ourselves?"

"Are you suggesting I am Ben?" asked Ron.

"I am suggesting you are aware we can all be Ben at times, my friend.

Avoidance Behavior

"I started running again a few years back—"

"That's was your first mistake," interrupted Ron with a chuckle.

Joe did not look amused. He continued. "At first, it hurt. But I stuck with it and it got better, plus I lost some weight and started feeling better about myself.

"For others, the desire to avoid the pain associated with starting to run may cause them not to exercise at all, and in the end, they will have to deal with the pain of poor health and degeneration.

"So how do you know when you attempt to avoid pain rather than manage it? Listen for phrases such as 'I know what I'm doing,' 'Don't fix what's not broken,' 'We've always done it this way,' or 'there's just no time for that now,' are evidence of pain avoidance. When you hear these comments, bells should go off in your head. Something should change and is likely being avoided either consciously or subconsciously. If you think any of these thoughts as you read, stop, and take time to reflect on why.

"Most people put off change so long that eventually the pain of their current procrastination becomes even greater than the discomfort of making the change would have been to begin with. It is my hope that through honesty and intentionality you will choose sustainable significance rather than procrastination—it's your choice."

Exercise: Reservations and Pain

Take a moment to review this section and reflect on your own "headspace." What reservations, biases, and other thoughts do you hold on to that prevent you from being all you know you can be?

- Write down any thoughts, behaviors, or chatter in your head today and put it on paper.
    - o What areas of shock or disbelief do you have?
    - o What new information or obstacles are you struggling to push through in your business today?
    - o What tendencies do you have when dealing with change and pain?
- When you start to stagnate, revisit this exercise and see if you are repeating past prohibitions of your mind. If so, STOP! Additionally, if you recognize new red flags (no matter how legitimate as they may or may not seem). Add them to this list.

Write down your *pain* related reservations(s) and details here

---

For further development, visit the workbook in the back or *The Q4 Quest* online.

Reservations 2 – Partiality

Personal Bias

"Behind every argument is someone's ignorance." - Louis D. Brandeis.

When we argue with others, especially over what we believe to be their best interest, we must ask ourselves the question, which one of us doesn't know the truth? Now, if we are struggling in our own minds with ourselves, the answer should be obvious. *The Q4 Quest*, if nothing else, establishes clarity. Without clarity, we are both ignorant and blind—two dangerous variables for seeking to live a Q4 life.

Let's consider ignorance first. I believe Mark Twain was right when he said, "Never argue with an idiot. They will drag you down to their level and beat you with experience." We are all idiots at times, or at least not as accurate as we like to think. For example, one famous study showed that over seventy percent of police eyewitness' convictions were overturned after DNA testing was introduced into the case. In other words, even people under oath in court who swore by their convictions were found to be wrong most of the time. Not only are our memories far less reliable than we think, but pride causes a phenomenon called confirmation bias.

Confirmation Bias

Confirmation bias means hearing what we want to hear and believing only what aligns with what we already think. The science world defines it as the tendency to interpret new evidence as confirmation of our existing beliefs or theories. Our Q4 Quest's confirmation bias, as a form of reservation, clogs our clarity and makes it dangerous, leading to flawed decision-making. For example, a business leader might come up with a new idea or direction for the company. Then he or she asks the team to crunch the numbers and do relevant market research to explore its feasibility. If this sounds right, think again. What just happened is a common form of confirmation bias. Any data collected tests only the potential level of effectiveness for the new option. An honest assessment of the data would have explored competing options, suggested alternative models, and the

The Q4 Quest for Financial Advisors

option of not doing anything at all. Try telling this person that not only is their idea not the best for the company, but someone else's competing idea tests more favorably for the company. Although reason might suggest they will listen to the new information for the betterment of all, including their own company, real-life confirmation bias often submits otherwise.

In life and financial planning, I have seen people of all levels of success and intelligence fall victim to this form of resistance. I have seen people who have and love annuities, and people who don't and hate them, both with little supporting reasoning. I have watched people hold on to bad stocks all the way to the bottom, thinking if they just wait until they come back they will be able to sell and that right now the money "is only lost on paper." Except the dollar value is the same today, regardless of what it might be invested in, so the smart money would consider the most appropriate investment for today. Even business tycoon and former Secretary of Treasury Andrew W. Mellon said, "There is no cause to worry. The high tide of prosperity will continue." This led many investors to follow his money into the stock market, despite evidence to the contrary. That was 1929, only a month before the stock market crash of the Great Depression. Pride does not discriminate.

(In the last twenty years, many people have told me how they timed the market correction of the early 2000s and the collapse of the Twin Towers, of the Global Financial Crises of 2008, and other outlandish claims along the way. I have also never met anyone who admitted that they invested and lost during those periods, despite the financial statistics to the contrary. That's partiality bias at its best).

Now, when it comes to building a practice, the same biases are at work. For example, when we first fall in love, all we notice are our partner's strengths, not to mention we feel that we walk on water. However, when that relationship heads a little south, all those little quirks that you once thought were so cute now become an insurmountable list of irritating flaws. This is the confirmation bias filter again, selectively allowing us only to see more of what we want to see and less of what we don't.

Joe paused for effect before adding "Ron, the significance of living a life inspired by our quest is that the process of perception is cyclical. If we think we are good, we are more likely to act well, and if we think we are broken, we tend to act broken. We all can get stuck in our own debilitating ideology such as, 'I know what I'm doing,' 'don't fix what's not broken,' 'we've always done it this way,' 'we've never done it like that before,' or 'there's just no time for that now.' Let these phrases be a warning to you, my brother."

Ron squirmed a bit in his seat. He knew he had said these statements many times as of late.

Joe continued. "But, do not worry, Ron, you're not alone. Let me explain."

We Believe Our Own Lies

"In the early 90s, researchers used DNA to back-test the accuracy of eyewitness testimony. The research proved conclusively that we are ALL wrong far more often than we like to believe.

"After studying hundreds of cases where people testified in court under oath to their eyewitness testimony, DNA discounted not 10 percent or even fifty percent of the testimony under oath, but over 70 percent were found to be in error about the witnesses' legal convictions.

"What's even more alarming is that even after the DNA results were presented with the cases proving that the witnesses were wrong, most of the witnesses still clung tight to their testimonies. "I don't care what the evidence says, I know what I saw," they would say. Regardless of the facts, most people cannot accept their perspective is wrong, even considering the overwhelming evidence."

Note to self: stop trying to change people's perspectives, especially on social media.

Confirmation bias is real. We all have it, and it appears likely that over 70 percent of what we think we know is wrong.

Exercise: Partiality Reservations

Take a moment to review this section and reflect on your own "headspace." What reservations, biases, and other thoughts do you hold onto that prevent you from being all you know you can be?

- Write down any thoughts, behaviors, or chatter in your head today and put it on paper.
- When you start to stagnate, revisit this exercise, and see if you are repeating past prohibitions of your mind. If so, STOP! if you recognize new red flags (as legitimate as they may seem). Add them to the list.

> Write down your *partiality* related reservations(s) and details here

For further development, visit the workbook section of this Quest and update your profile online.

Reservations 3 – Pride

Ego - Blinded by the 'Lies'

Joe leaned in, "When we admit that we have imperfections and mistakes in our lives we are also admitting that we have been wrong. For many, our pride can't reconcile that."

"I am not that bad," Ron insisted.

"I have raised a family, built a successful business, sent my kids to school, and still saved some along the way. I am proud of what I have accomplished."

"Listen Ron, pride is perhaps the biggest lie we face. We often defend our choices with a list of accomplishments."

"Yes, we have a right to be proud of the accomplishments in our lives. However, the healthier perspective is to be appreciative of all that has been bestowed upon us, rather than about how great we are, or how much better we are than those with less.

"Think about it like this. How many amazing musicians have dedicated their lives to their skill and barely make a living in seedy bars in Nashville or New Orleans? Now, consider the entertainers with a fraction of their talent who blow up and become multi-millionaires because of cultural winds of happenstance and the material machine of capitalism?

"The point is, as hard as it may be to swallow, we must all be careful to not think our successes had too much to do with our talent and hard work without the acknowledgment of grace, or help from above. Of course, this is not to say you didn't work hard, or you don't have talent.

"If you are still unsure about this premise, I assure you that you are not alone. This client never believed it either. His pride relentlessly blinded him. "I worked my tail off to get here," he would say, and I believe he worked hard. However, I also believe that the bubblegum boy bands also worked their tails off to ride the consumer roller coaster as well, but it was something bigger than them that put them on the ride, to begin with."

"Noted" Ron added with reluctant sarcasm.

The Q4 Quest is a reality check and a hard, honest look in the mirror. Don't forget that, as my friend did. My friend continues to hold his prideful convictions, and he continues to struggle to this day. Perhaps that will always be his cross to bear?

Honest Desire

Consider what Mathew Shultz said: "Our biggest struggle as human beings is to project ourselves as something that society has deemed admirable or likable instead of being honest." If you applied the previous lesson on clarity and confirmation bias, you are ready to "get real" with yourself. It takes humility, the opposite of pride, to be honest with yourself. The Q4 Quest requires humble authenticity in your introspection so that you can have authentic success with your execution.

As a trainer of financial advisors, I can't count how many supposed "sales gurus" I have met who bragged about how forward-thinking they were while simultaneously teaching the same rubbish—1980s techniques that commoditized people at best even then. This is hardly sales, and it's not the Q4 Quest.

Most salespeople have been taught sales are a "numbers game." Kiss enough frogs and you will find your next prince. Unfortunately, while there is some truth to this, this also diminishes the meaning of our profession a bit. With the billions of people in the world, I would rather spend time with the right fifty to one hundred than on building a mousetrap focused on the law of large numbers. Shouldn't we focus on treating people right and solving their needs with valuable solutions? This is quality over quantity.

What's more, shouldn't we be doing the same thing in our personal lives? Looking for quality solutions, it becomes almost funny, in a sad way, how lost everyone appears once we really see it. The good and sometimes frustrating news is that once you see it, you can't un-see it. (This can make receiving antiquated advice hard to listen to). Once you become sustainably significant, the paradigm of the masses becomes distant static. Sure, you might forget to live Q4 at times, but you won't ever again unsee it.

By way of example, consider my now-surfer friend, Chad. Formerly a traditional 9-5 suit wearing financial advisor right out of college. He is a go-getter, pushing himself hard to be the best at everything he does. Unfortunately, he has also been sold the societal bill of lies. Chad's well-intended manager has been training him to fit into the same broken paradigm he inherited from his manager, who likely learned the same from his manager.

Chad's manager often brags today about how he was a drummer growing up and throughout college, but like so many he put that on hold to focus on career, family, and to do the responsible thing as he was taught. Unfortunately, decades later he barely touches the drums despite the small voice inside buried under piles of literal and metaphorical paperwork. The fire has all but gone out as he plays by society's lie. The lie that so many fall victim that we have to exchange a part of our spark to conform to a predefined definition of success. For example, Chad's gift and his passion is surfing, and he was good enough in college to cover all his expenses and then some through sponsorships and tournaments. Here's the problem: like his manager, there is no time for it today as he has been guided to put it on hold as he focuses on his career. It wasn't in his job description these days, and he had relegated his passion to an immature hobby for which he didn't have time.

If business was Chad's passion, this might be great, but it wasn't. Like so many of us, Chad bought the lie that if he took a break to focus and plug away, eventually this dry season of work would slow down, and he would have time to surf again. Now, as anyone who has bought this lie will tell you, time will catch up with you and you will never find your way back. The body will breakdown, and the joy deferred will eat away at your soul. Don't put off joy as tomorrow may not come.

Thanks to Q4, Chad is a business consultant for small surf shops and has traded in suits and board rooms for shorts and surfboards! What is your surfboard?

The Jones's

"So, where do so many get lost?" Asked Ron.

"Many people, especially earlier in life, fall into the material game known as "keeping up with the Joneses." I've met them, the proverbial Joneses—they're okay, but their dog is really yippy! Plus, they live under very heavy and constant pressure, constantly striving to reach some imaginary and self-prescribed benchmark of success defined by titles, appearances, and possessions. The Joneses and their disciples allow the world to define their game. But what about the things that last like happiness, relationship, and love? Of course, we know there will always be someone with a bigger house, more money, or a faster car, and the end of this road is bleak.

"However, we often miss that this path is not just limited to material things; it also manifests in our ambitions. Those imaginary benchmarks are often born of youth and lies we have told ourselves about others' expectations and are not fueled by any authentic hunger. We have all had dreams or aspirations that sounded good when we said them—"I want to lose weight this year," or "I want to make improvements in my career or my family," only to die on the vine when it comes time to discipline and commitment. Commitment, after all, is sticking to your goals after the fire you had when you made them fades."

Thinking about this in his own life Ron added, "I have been known to get all excited at times about new business ideas only to lose interest when the daily grind overwhelms me."

This is when we find out if we are true to ourselves when we profess our goals, or if we are just telling ourselves what the Joneses would expect us to say? After all, if we truly care about something, we need not be told to make it happen; if anything, we need to be told to slow down and find balance. This honesty, coupled with our new clarity, lays the groundwork for following our Q4 Quest."

Living the Dream

Even someone who has been up and down the corporate ladder would say, "Anything short of genuine living, even if we can pull it off for a little while, will eventually revert to our authentic self, driven by our most sincere desires rather than someone else's. In other words, after Halloween we all go back to wearing normal work clothes. The same is true about when we try to overhaul our business practices overnight. It can't last, and what's worse is the next time around we are weighed down by added feelings of defeat, depression, or despair over our newfound shortcomings. In short, being something, anything other than what we were made to be is painful, difficult, and not much fun. In the end, we will only end up more like an apple tree fruitlessly straining to produce peaches!

Think about it like this. Have you ever asked a person how they are doing and had them respond, 'Living the dream?' A friend of mine says this so much it got me thinking about what this phrase really means.

Maybe it's about a certain quality of life or being able to provide and protect for the people that matter most? It likely has something to do with enjoying what we get to do every day. Something to do with living life purposefully. No matter how we describe it, 'living the dream' clearly has something to do with winning in life. Something to do with joy and happiness.

"Happiness is overrated," is what my neighbor always says, to which I (Chris) respond like clockwork, "Said an unhappy person!" Happiness is great, but remember, it's not the ultimate objective. Think of it as a temporary steppingstone to joy, but one that's worth a closer look. I once asked a room full of people how many of them thought they might be genuinely happy. The majority answer was about half.

Then I came across the "happiness index," and yes, it's a real thing. According to the 2013 poll, only one in three adults is genuinely happy. Said another way, two out of three people are wailing around unhappily. Let that sink in. Even with all the self-help books, consultants, counselors, and life coaches telling us what to do to so few people are living happily.

Typically, when a few people are wrong, they might need to look at themselves, but when the majority is wrong, the problem is clearly systemic. As a society, we have gone astray, and there sure is a serious disconnect today. *The Q4 Quest* is contrarian and all about breaking away from these broken, stagnant paradigms.

The Q4 Quest is about leaving bad habits behind by focusing on all that is good. All that inspires us and brings us happiness. To embrace a Q4 life, we must be honest down to our core about who and what we care about, and what we don't. Otherwise, we are likely to fall back into old habits.

Take the top two areas that, according to consumer reports, our society wants to improve the most: weight loss and money management. What can we learn from these industries that might help personally? Weight loss companies anticipate that most of us will begin with a destination, such as the ideal image or target weight in mind, rather than a journey, or lifestyle change. The result? We fail. Most people will never change, and those who do usually cannot sustain their new physique for long. That's just how we are wired.

The industry makes millions knowing that if people go about things wrong, they can continue to resell most of us the same fad diet again next year in a new wrapper and make billions. I (Chris) have both P90X versions and Body Beast, not to mention multiple weight benches and dumbbells on my shelf collecting dust, but I still haven't grown any stronger! Simply put, I liked the idea of being healthier more than the idea of becoming healthier. Said another way—I had a dream, not a sincere motivation.

What about money management, an area I have personal experience in? Financial professionals, ideally at least, want their clients to be better off, and in most cases, these professionals work hard to achieve this. These professionals have the difficult task of selling change to a world afraid of change, and prudence to a world that seeks pleasure. They promote the virtues of patience in a society craving instant gratification and provide invisible security to a culture seeking material gains. Financial professionals are paid to wade through compliance issues, increasingly complicated paperwork, and ever-changing regulations while also seeking to develop meaningful relationships with people who generally spend more time planning a vacation than for retirement.

These professionals manage the pressures of negative sales stigma and shaming headlines while continuing to fight and rise above the noise and deliver real value that makes a business stronger, families more financially secure, and communities empowered.

Yet, with all these professionals and reports showing how high a priority prudent planning is on the average Americans to-do list, why do most of us still tend to run from the topic altogether? Why do so many avoid doing what they say they want with their own words? Why do nearly one out of four Americans have less than five-thousand dollars earmarked for retirement, and why do millions have little insurance to adequately protect their families? Simple. We like the dream of "being" okay more than the work of "becoming" okay.

To be frank, we often lie to ourselves, and deep down, we know it. Over time, these self-delusions accumulate, and our souls can become burdened and heavy. So, what should we do about it, you ask? How do we flip the script? Easy. We stop lying to ourselves, and we start living authentically.

Exercise: Pride Reservations

Take a moment to review this section and reflect on your own "headspace." What reservations, biases, and other thoughts do you hold on to that prevent you from being all you know you can be?

- Write down any thoughts, behaviors, or chatter in your head today and put it on paper.
    - o   Where have you said, "I've always done it that way"?
    - o   Where have you said, "It worked that way before"?
    - o   Where have you refused to take advice that has come from multiple sources?
- When you start to stagnate, revisit this exercise, and see if you are repeating past prohibitions of your mind. If so, STOP! if you

recognize new red flags (as legitimate as they may seem). Add them to the list.

> Write down your *pain* related reservations(s) and details here

For further development, visit the workbook in the back or *The Q4 Quest* online.

Final Thoughts

With an inquisitive look on his face Ron leaned in and said, "But I am still not quite getting what Q4 is Joe? What does all this talk about perspective have to do with the secret to building a better business- a better life?"

Joe just let it roll off of his back. "There will be plenty of time to see this more clearly I promise but you have got trust me. So, for now know this, transformation begins when we renew our minds and let go of the mistakes and lies instilled by the world around us. The two biggest mistakes we make are a) trusting in the ways of the world, look around and see how that is going, and b) trusting in ourselves. Our pride and biases cloud are vision and ability to see the clear path to abundance right in front of us"

"Okay Joe. You have got me on the hook. I will keep an open mind through all this and try to set my judgement and skepticism aside"

"Then let's keep going!"

Q3

SITUATION

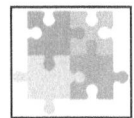

The 4Ps of Situation Covers:

- **Pasion**
  Exercise: Pasion Assessment
- **Personality**
  Exercise: Myers-Briggs
  Exercise: Finder/Binder/Grinder/Minder
- **Personal Story**
  Exercise: Past – Meaningful Event or Motivator
  Exercise: Present – Magnetic Marketing Bio
- **Professional Resources**
  Exercise: Resources – Time (EPH)
  Exercise: Resources – Money
  [A) AUM, B) Run Rate, and C) Reinvestment]
  Exercise: Resources – Relationships

Now, for a little less philosophy and a little more action.

This third section is more of an assessment and inventory than the previous sections. As we walk together through the 4Ps of your situation, Passions, Personality, Personally Story, and Professional Inventory, we will start formulation of the map towards your Q4.

Situation 1 - Passions

Consider the Flea Trainers

Papa Joe began his discussion about passions with another off-the-wall parable. Looking at Ron, he asked, "Did you know that there really are flea trainers?"

"Flea Trainers?" asked Ron.

"Yes, flea, trainers! Let me explain. You see, fleas are trained by putting them in a cardboard box with a clear top on it. The fleas jump up, hitting their heads repeatedly until eventually, they begin jumping lower to avoid hitting their heads on the transparent lid. While the fleas can't see the clear lid, the headaches are still there, and they've become conditioned to lower their performance to avoid the headaches. Interestingly, when you remove the lid, the fleas continue to jump at the conditioned, lower height. Predictable yet strange.

"The reality is that the fleas won't escape their captivity because they believe they can't. They have been conditioned to stay in the transparent and non-existent paradigm by the restraints of their misunderstanding minds. In short, they have conformed to the world and now settle for the lowest common denominator rather than their personal best, and their 'reality' has no resemblance to actual reality."

Stepping outside our dialogue for a moment, as a trainer and coach for financial advisors myself I, Chris, have seen far too many otherwise amazing professionals with gobs of untapped potential squelch their business because of the invisible lid in their minds. Believing that their business must fit the restraints of the industry at large, most practices look the same across the country: average and unattractive.

Not only does this make them less fun to operate, but they also become less magnetic to the would-be client, and the business suffers. Here in the state of Florida, according to PayScale.com, the average income for a financial advisor is $42,000 a year. Compare that to those who jump outside the box and beyond the lid of conformity, which is earning hundreds of thousands if not millions of dollars for similar work.

If you are reading this, the chances are you are not average. So why let the "lid of the average" define your potential in any career or area of life?

You can choose to do what everyone around you thinks is best, or you can choose to soar with the best and live a life of unprecedented sustainable significance. Who are you, and what are you passionate about that could help you break through the lid to new heights in your business and your life?

Exercise: Passion Assessment

Using the following short exercise inventory, list your unique passions and gifts. Consider how are you using them (or not) in your quest?

1. *Goosebumps*: Those endeavors that give you metaphorical goosebumps, such as surfing or playing drums.
2. *Jump Ups*: These are activities or aspects of your life that excite you and get you jumping out of bed in the morning, such as helping other surfers reach their potential.
3. *Fun times and Hobbies*: Here you might list skills/hobbies that come naturally, and the ones you enjoy.

Goosebumps	Jump-ups	Fun times / hobbies

- Looking at these questions, what things have you let go of that you wish you were still doing?
- Now, in what ways can you reframe your game to include more of your gifts and passions?
- Now, look at the significance that your past can play in your present and your future.

For further development, visit the workbook in the back or *The Q4 Quest* online.

Situation 2 - Personality

"In the Marine Corps," Chris says, "we often assigned tasks to people based on natural ability. For example, the fast guys might become runners, while the biggest guys might carry additional ammo or larger weapons. The smaller guys often were sent on recon patrols or to flush out caves and tunnels."

In business and in life, we should apply a similar common sense. The extroverts might likely "play in traffic" by networking to meet new prospective clients, while the introverts might build a more magnetic approach to business acquisition.

"So, do you know your personality type?" Joe asked Ron. "Do you know how to use your personality type to drive your business success?"

"I am not sure," Ron paused.

"Through science," Joe explained, "we can prevent mistakes like being the introvert who believes they must follow an outbound practice model to succeed at sales. Ouch! Let's use the Myers-Briggs test here as our foundation, to determine your sales style and then explore how to use this information to catapult your potential."

Myers Briggs

In the 1940s, Isabel Briggs Myers and her mother, Katherine Briggs, expanded on the psychological works of Carl Jung, giving birth to the now-famous Myers-Briggs test. This test, still used today, divides all people by personality into one of sixteen personality types by dividing four core preferences into two camps as follows:

- World Focus (E / I): Extroverts prefer to focus on the outer world, while Introverts prefer to focus on their inner world.
- Information (S / N): Sensors prefer to focus on facts at hand, while the Intuitive prefer to extrapolate meaning.
- Decision Making (T / F): Thinkers prefer to make decisions through logical consistency, while Feelers first look at the people and special circumstances to apply to reason.

- Structure (J / P): Judgers prefer to do things the way they have been told, or the way they have always been done, while Perceivers are open to new information and look for new ways to do things.

After taking the placement test associated with Myers-Briggs, a person will be labeled as primarily one type more than all others. That's not to say we do not all have elements of each type within us. We are all merely discerning which personality-type we are prone to lean to more than another.

There are also no right or wrong answers, and one type is not better than another. Knowing your type can help a person to focus more on their strengths and avoid occupations that call on areas that are changing for us. Today, corporations, phycologists, and academics around the world use this tool in career placement, relational compatibility, personal counseling, and team building.

Now it's your turn.

Exercise: Personality Type

Using the following resources, determine your personality type and record it here. _____.

Visit https://www.16personalities.com/free-personality-test and take your free personality test. (Be honest—there are no wrong answers).

To further explore or simply record your personality type, visit the workbook in the back or *The Q4 Quest* online.

Finder – Binder – Grinder – Minder (FBGM)

Knowing your personality type might be fun, but to make it meaningful, you must do something with that information. Finder / Binder / Grinder / Minder, or FBGM, puts that information into a practical application, and any organization from one to thousands serious about increasing sales should take an honest look at themselves and their situation. Using the personality type you identified with through the Myers Briggs test, find yourself on the following chart.

Sales Teams / Aptitudes		*Applying Myers-Briggs*
(E _ F _) Extroverted – Feeler – (generally Perceiving) **FINDER** The Traditional *Hunter* great at New Business Development • ENFP: (Champion / Campaigner)* • ESFP: (Performer)* • ENFJ: (Giver / Protagonist)* • ESFJ: (Caregiver / Counsel)*	**(E _ T _)** Introverted – Thinker (generally Judging) **BINDER** The Traditional *Closer* great at Sealing The Deal • ENTJ: (Commander)* • ESTJ: (Director / Executive) • ENTP: (Debater / Entrepreneur) • ESTP: (Persuader)*	
(I _ T _) Introverted – Thinker (generally Judging) **GRINDER** The Traditional *Workhorse* for Managing Available Accounts • INTJ: (Architect)* • ISTJ: (Inspector / Logistician)* • INTP: (Thinker) • ISTP: (Crafter / Virtuoso)	**(I _ F _)** Introverted – Feeler (generally Perceiving) **MINDER** The Traditional *Glue* to any Repeatably Referrable Sales Practice • INFP: (Mediator)! • ISFP: (Artist / Adventurer)! • INFJ: (Advocate)! • ISFJ: (Protector / Defender)*	

* = High Probability of Success In This Role   ! = Be Cautious In Any Sales Role

Which type are you? A Finder or a Binder? Perhaps a more methodical Grinder or Minder?

Let us take a closer look. Remember that we all have elements of other personalities. There are also certainly exceptions to every rule. If you are drawn to a position that seems to be outside of your traditional type, that merely means being conscious of how your personal characteristics might influence you in that role.

1. *Finder* – A traditional sales Hunter is great at developing new business. Finders can also close and service clients, but often get bogged down in the details. For these reasons, Finders should consider adding a service component to begin with, followed by a Binder as the growth warrants.
2. *Binder* – A traditional sales Binder or "closer" is great at sealing the deal. Binders can also hunt and service, but often get burned out or overwhelmed with the day-to-day and should consider adding a service component to begin with, followed by one or more Finders as the growth warrants.
3. *Grinder* – A Grinder is a traditional workhorse on the service side of a sales team. Grinders are great at developing, maintaining, and improving systems and processes and ideal for an established business or part of a disciplined two-sided team. Grinders can also close sales if necessary, but will avoid hunting if possible, through creative strategies to accomplish sales such as marketing,

cross-selling, and retention. They should partner with a Finder or Binder as soon as possible and look to add a Minder as growth warrants.
4. *Minder* – The glue to any relationship-driven practice falling on the service side of a sales team is the Minder. Minders are great at duplicating best clients through acts of sincere appreciation. They are necessary for growing any established business, but also make great partners to a disciplined two-sided team. Minders can also close sales if necessary, but are not too eager to try. For these reasons, they should partner with a Finder or Binder as soon as possible and look to add a Grinder as growth warrants.

For you to get the most out of your personality type, we often advise teaming with complimenting personality types. When a Finder/Binder teams with a Grinder/Minder, 1+1 can = 3 or 4 or more.

Do you honestly have a person gifted in each of the respective areas working following a clearly defined repeatable process? If not, consider that your alternative is to simply do more of what you are doing and hope that sheer tenacity will compensate for your lack of structure and that you won't burn out in the process by being forced to spread your skills and time too thin.

On the other hand, if you take the time to learn from this and rearrange your relationships and resources accordingly, your business and your life will become inheritably fun and wildly successful.

Consider this example:

- A finder, an extrovert who loves to meet new people, wakes up hungry to hunt. They can quickly perceive their surroundings and adjust their behavior accordingly to open new relationships and potential business opportunities. This person is a great salesperson and also has the skills to be a "closer" and to "service" clients. However, in doing all these tasks, their capacity for maximizing their chief strength is minimized, and so is their peak potential.
- So, they team up with a binder. This person is also great at sales, however, they can get burned out with the day-to-day discipline needed to hunt consistently. This person has chess-like ability

to close deals and has no problem being in pushy or awkward situations. They often say things like, "I could close anyone if I just had more people to get in front of." Their problem is their pride will not usually permit them to partner with a Finder, and their inability to bring in consistent business means they often struggle maintaining the routine necessary to add a service component to their practice. In turn, they grow much slower than their sales skills would suggest they could.

- The grinder is an intelligent introvert that can see things others cannot. They can take a sales process to new heights with little effort if they can find a place to fit in where they are appreciated. This type is usually too passive to be the front-end salesperson, so they often get overlooked and ignored if they are even invited to the party at all. However, a practice that allows this person to uncover ancillary opportunities, cross-sells, and strategic alliances can often double revenue with the existing amount of relationships by working smarter rather than harder.
- The last part of the team and the conveyer belt towards success is the minder. This person is also an inside (administrative) type of person, but their ability to put the "love" in the business is crucial. They make clients feel good by remembering birthdays and anniversaries. They even know what the clients want to do on vacation and where they went. Often teams hire a person for an administrative role and assume they will do these things, and that is often not the case. They can be as polar as a college professor and an elementary teacher. However, if implemented properly, the minder is often the catalyst to taking a good business through the stratosphere because they will love on the best clients so much that referrals and centers of influence will flock to your practice as you duplicate top-tier clients repeatedly.

Exercise: FBGM Aptitude

> Now, using the previous personality tests, record your FBGM aptitude here.

- What personality types do you have around you that could be leveraged to catapult your practice?
- What types do you still need to find, add, or develop to your process to maximize your success?
- What actions might you take to start strengthening your team?

To further explore and record your FBGM aptitude, visit the workbook in the back or *The Q4 Quest* online.

Situation 3 - Personal Stories

Back at the diner, Papa Joe took a sip of his water. Then he took a deep breath in and told Ron, "Take a breather, my friend. I have another short story I want to share with you."

Ron knew by now that each story had a purpose, so without hesitation he sat back and got comfortable.

The Bus

Joe began. "It was a hot Florida afternoon, and the school day had had just ended. My friend, Rick, a teacher, had just finished herding the children onto the school bus to send them home and was heading for a happy hour when he heard a loud bang.

"Rick ran along with a group of other teachers to the commotion. When he got there, it was like a surreal movie scene. Children were on the ground and there was metal, books, and blood everywhere. He heard screaming, but everything seemed to be moving in slow motion. Or maybe fast forward. It's hard to tell.

"Soon the crying was accompanied by the sounds of cars and sirens, and a man suddenly approached him who seemed to be an official. He asked if Rick was a teacher.

"'Yes, I had five students on that bus,'" Rick replied. Then the man asked if Rick could make an identification. Again, Rick responded, saying, 'Yes, I can.' Together they walked to what appeared to be a triage point. There were blankets covering multiple, small, lifeless bodies. Removing the blanket, Rick saw Tommy and Matthew intertwined together—one black and one white—both gone, just like that.

"'I'll never, ever forget that image and what it meant to me,'" Rick cried.

"This event has driven Rick to accomplish many great things in education and impact thousands of students. But what does it have to do with his planning or decision making today? Simple, this event has also been the source of much pressure. Haunted by common thoughts like, 'What could I have done?' or 'If I only did something different,' Rick's entire journey has been shaped by the pressure to do more for children.

Nothing is ever enough. Every decision one makes is about what more one can do.

"Now, think about this in the context of financial planning, for example. Retirement discussions for Rick are out of the question because in his mind, at least currently, it would mean turning his back on more children. Couple that with pride and age, and that he thinks no one can do what he can do, so succession planning becomes a four-letter word.

"Now, add in confirmation bias because past successes have encouraged him to over-trust his own belief system regardless of evidence to the contrary, and what you get is a man unable to receive guidance without resistance and maybe even animosity. As they say, it's the proverbial bus you didn't expect that can get you."

So, what about your past?

Is there a bus coming that needs to be addressed so you can move on to a healthy place? Perhaps a death, an illness, a trauma, or even a great success that you could plot on your own timeline that will influence your decision-making process? What might that do to your decision making?

The fact is, you are working to develop your practice, and that suggests you are probably already good, perhaps even great at what you do, and now on a trajectory for sustainable significance. So, the question then becomes, what makes you great, and how might you pass that wisdom on to those you serve? Just like our story of the bus, think about what trials you have overcome that could now attract others to your unique insights and expertise like moths to a flame.

Exercise: Personal Past – Part A

The following exercise will help you to pull out a defining event or theme that has shaped how you tell your story today. The difference between a basic biography and a magnetic marketing statement is found in your ability to tell your story well. Our private clients often spend hours, weeks, even months perfecting this process, but you can begin your story right here.

- What trial or event have you overcome that fuels your passion or practice today?
- Can you define your event in just a few words?
- Now, being more specific, how does this event still shape who you are today?
- What audience might be most attracted to your story and insight?
- How do you capture that in your business, marketing, and other relationships?

> Complete your "past" exercise here.

To further explore and record your past, visit the workbook in the back or *The Q4 Quest* online.

Exercise: Present Story – Part B (Be Magnetic)

Now, it's time to get magnetic.

Using all that we have learned so far, write your own magnetic marketing biography.

- Perhaps you will only need to rework what existing generic information into more provoking and personal information. Others may want to start fresh with all this added introspection.
- Remember to make it personal because people are more likely to seek out relationships with people they can relate to.

On no more than one or two pages, write your concise but thorough biography, remembering to include highlights from the following:

- Who matters most to you?
  (Consider including multiple tiers from your six-tiers of relational influence).
- What matters most to you?
  (Consider highlighting your personal vision and mission as well as any unique professional priorities).
- Your relevant passions and gifts.
  (Consider anything that might make you relatable to your ideal audiences).
- Your past.
  (Any events that make you approachable by your ideal audiences).

Complete your "bio" exercise here.

To further explore and record your past, visit the workbook in the back or *The Q4 Quest* online.

Situation 4 - Professional Resources

On more than one occasion, I have taught classes on how to double your business in a year without any cold prospecting or expensive seminars. I have learned that it works. It's possible to do in a very short amount of time, and most people will never take the time to do it because they are too busy with a self-appointed niche that we call "playing work."

"Imagine this," said Joe, "you are at a conference, workshop, or lunch-and-learn with a local sponsor and professionals from multiple disciplines, including investment, insurance, planning, tax, and legal. Everyone there came because they have established businesses, but also have the capacity and desire to grow considerably, and hopefully without much wasted time or money.

"Throughout the class, we teach, as we often do, tips for cost-effective time management (time), ways to build more efficient marketing programs (money), and immediate steps for duplicating your best clients through existing relationships (relationships). Without a doubt, the most important resources we have, as anyone with any business experience can tell you, are our relationships. Yet strangely, most people spend more time on managing their money (marketing) than they do on deepening these positional relationships. Let me be more specific.

"Before we break for lunch, we tell the attendees we have an exercise that requires them to divide themselves by their niche disciplines—accountants with accountants, brokers with brokers, and so on. Then like an arthritic game of musical chairs, we sit them all at tables with professionals from complimenting cross-disciplines. Think about it. At each table is a financial planner, a banker, an insurance agent, a tax professional, and a legal counselor.

"In this example, I tell them the doors will be locked until they have all looked at their top 10 clients with the rest of the table (without names, of course, to protect client confidentiality). What they are looking for is what we call "coordination gaps" or areas where there may be inconsistencies across the aisle. This includes conflicting beneficiaries on documents and wills, unfunded trusts, or no contact information for planners. These areas can unwittingly cost a client hundreds, maybe thousands, or millions of dollars in some cases. Think about it. When was the last time that most clients had their whole team look at this picture together from a financial, tax, legal, and insurance perspective? When was the last time you have done this for your top clients? We have found that the difference between having work done by each of these professionals and having it coordinated as well as possible can mean thousands, if not millions of dollars saved or earned, not to mention greater clarity and confidence. In other words, it creates more opportunities to move the needle for your best relationships.

"These proactive cross-disciplinary meetings also create reciprocal relationships coming from the other professionals at the table who can now see you in a more complementary and competent professional role. In other words, they are confident introducing you to their more holistic relationships, and you each gain new relationships that mirror your existing top clients. Assuming each of the five people at the table above had five to ten relationships to share with their new "A-Team," that represents twenty-five to fifty new A-tier clients without any marketing. What difference might fifty new A relationships this year mean to your existing business? Even twenty-five? Or only ten?"

"That would be life-changing, Joe!" Ron said, eager to get started.

"You got it, Ron, but before we race out and embrace ourselves, let's do the foundational prep-work necessary to make sure you are prepared to not only best represent your own practice, but also to best serve any relationships you may share. So, let us take a look at how to best manage your three professional resources: time, money, and relationships.

Resources: time	Resources: money	Resources: relationships
Exercise: EPH	Exercise: AUM / Run Rate	Positional segmentation
Time allocation	Cashflow	Professional influencers
Work-life balance	Valuation	Personal relationships

Time

There is only so much time in a day. If you want to earn more, you can either work harder or smarter. If you are like most business owners and financial advisors, you are already working hard and have little bandwidth left to work harder, so the choice is made for you. If this is you, then you must begin to work smarter, and that begins by knowing what you are worth per hour. After all, if you do not know what an hour of your time is worth to you, then how will you know what you need to charge each client to reach your revenue goals?

There are many ways to calculate this number, and the more complex your business structure and employees, the more complex your calculations may need to be, but the basic math works like this.

Divide the amount of income you project earning for this year by the amount of hours worked in the year. (2,000 represents fifty weeks at forty hours per week doing client engagement).

Example: _____$150,000___ / 2,000 = ___$75_____ per hour.

Now, how many hours does a typical client take?

That depends on your specialty, demographic, and service model, but as a rule-of-thumb, the average A client takes twelve to eighteen hours a year to service, including travel, prep, review, and service calls. (Precisely why a solo practitioner or small practice does not have room to properly serve more than about 100 clients at a time and still have time to manage the other business activities essential to managing a practice).

Early in your career, it may have been a race to get your first clients, but as you grow, that sprint becomes a marathon, and the tools that made you a success early on are not the same tools you will need to refine to sustain new success.

Exercise: Resources – Time

Take a moment now to find your own target EPH (earnings per hour).

- Divide the amount of income you project earning this year by the number of hours you anticipate working. (2,000 represents fifty weeks at forty hours per week)

    Example: _____ / 2,000 = ___$_____ per hour.

Now, how many hours does a typical client take? Perhaps you have multiple service models? Find an average if necessary but focus on A-clients. (Average 'A' client takes 12-15 hours a year to serve.)

Using the previous example. What is your minimum target revenue per client (not adjusting for operational expenses)?

75 x 15 = _____ $_____

- **How many clients can you serve in 2000 hours leaving time for operations?** _____

- **How many clients do you have?** _____

- **How many clients pay you what you are worth?** _____

- **Do you need to have room for more clients currently or a need for less?**

These relationships represent those you allow to hold you back from your growth potential. You can resolve to stay where you are in your business or make a plan to move them up or out of your practice. (You should not feel as bad about moving on than you do about not having the necessary bandwidth to properly serve, provide for, and protect those who you care so much about).

In our private coaching, we also review how our professional hours are allocated compared to our goals and personal strengths, as well as a high-level review or work-life balance. However, time management begins by knowing and charging your target EPH.

Update your profile now, and for further development visit the workbook section of this Quest and update your profile online.

Money

Time and money are two sides of the same coin, and one impacts the other. To help you make sound decisions with your business, it is imperative, much like financial planning, to know where you are, where you are going, and how you are getting there. For new businesses, this section can be more challenging, however, for practices with a few years under their belts, these are perfect exercises to begin managing for growth rather than just running full speed and hoping for the best!

Exercise: Resources – Money

Take a moment now to find your growth rate by assets and then by income.

This section is a three-part exercise. A) Using the following chart as a guide, begin with a simple calculation of your existing assets, and projected growth rates.

A) AUM Forecasting

Net New Asset Number. (New assets less withdraws, transfers, markets, and attrition)	Example	You
Assets Under Management (AUM) at the beginning of LAST year:	$22,000,000	
AUM at the end of the Year:	$31,000,000	
Growth Rate in terms of a percentage % (Increase ÷ Original Number × 100):	41%	
(AUM) beginning of THIS year (Same as end of last year):	$31,000,000	
Growth Rate assuming previous years %:	$43,681,818	
Adjust for AUM lost each year due to transfers, deaths, RMD's, and other anticipated withdraws:	-$3,000,000	
AUM Trend	$40,681,818	
Adjust for anticipated market movement in your forecasting (Add or subtract %):	5%	
Forecasted AUM at Year End:	$42,715,909	
Increase	38%	

With this information, you can project next year's growth based on your situation.

Now B) by determining your run rate, that is the amount of revenue you earn off each dollar invested with you (as an average), you can also project your cash flow.

B) Run rate and this year's forecasted revenue.

	Run Rate (Target .80 - 1.00)	Example	You
	Last Year Total Commission as Gross Dealer Concession (GDC):	$140,000	
	AUM at the end of the Year:	$31,000,000	
	Run Rate (GDC / AUM)	0.45%	
	Forecasted AUM (From Above)	$42,715,909	
	GDC based on current Run Rate	$192,911	
	Payout (Grid rate)	70%	
	Net Earning before Expenses	$135,037	

In our private coaching, we spend more time on strategies for increasing run rates while improving your client's realized value.

To start, update your profile now, and for further development visit the workbook section of this Quest and update your profile online.

C) Reinvestment (rules-of-thumb) 50/30/20 rule

Now we come to the third and final part of this section: reinvestment rules-of-thumb. Building a budget is outside the scope of this book and may not be necessary given the audience. However, what is necessary is remembering that the business is both a lifestyle and an investment, and should, at a minimum, follow the 50/30/20 rule.

This means that 50% or revenue should be considered for needs, including base salaries and business expenses. 30% should be considered for business wants, including marketing (including seminars and client events), equipment, and improving infrastructure, with 20% being put into savings, including operating funds, insurance, and succession.

	Reinvestment Rules-of-Thumb	Example	You
	Net Earning before Expenses	$135,037	
	50% - needs (Salaries and Expenses)	$67,519	
	30% - wants (Marketing, New Equipment, Infrastructure)	$40,511	
	20% - savings (operating funds, insurance, and succession)	$27,007	

- Any revenue that exceeds early projections can be taken as a bonus above the base salary or reinvested into business growth or both.

We often find that many young practices extract too much money to maintain salaries, and then struggle to reinvest in proper marketing, staff, and infrastructure. These practices often do well until they do not, and once they start to sink, there are not enough oars to stay afloat, and they go under or change careers.

In our private coaching, we address this in detail. For our disciplined clients serious about treating their career as a business and not a sales marathon, we also spend more time on monitoring marketing activities for maximizing return on investment (ROI) and minimizing costs of acquisition (COA).

For now, build a strong foundation and update your profile. For further development, visit the workbook section of this Quest and update your profile online.

Relationships

"Okay, Ron," said Joe, "now think back to a time when you just knew you were the best person for a job, whatever it was. Not necessarily a career either, but a role that needed to be filled for the benefit of others. It could have been as simple as being a Scout leader, a minister, or a youth coach. You were not there because you had to be or needed the money. You were there because you wanted to be and because others benefited from your gifts. They were glad you were there because you could effortlessly be everything they needed and more. This situation was simply about being passionately human. It was about the relationship. It was part of why you are here. In these types of situations, how did you carry yourself?"

"With confidence!" Ron said without hesitation.

"Exactly, and I bet you had had joy, energy, and ease as well, didn't you?"

"Yeah, things just came easy in those situations."

"Exactly, Ron, and this is exactly what we are looking for more of. As a consultant, I can tell you that when I am off the clock, or at least unconcerned with the clock and the commission, that is when I work my best. When we stop thinking of everything as a numbers game and start seeing everyone as a true relationship and opportunity to serve, energy starts to flow, and great things happen. In short, the Q4 Quest comes from a proper understanding that we are all in one business . . . the relationship business. Now, you just need to learn how to manage these relationships."

The Q4 Quest looks at our relationships through three lenses: personal, professional, and positional.

- Personal relationships are those closest to you, those in your inner circle, like family, friends, and any of your closest business partners. You may recall the relationship mapping exercises earlier in your quest. We started there for a reason because relationships are your number one resource. If I took all your money away, but you had relationships, you would be okay in the end. However, if I isolate you from everyone forever, even with all the money in the world, you would still be in prison.
- Professional relationships are those outside your key employees. These may be referral partners from a networking group or accountants who know and utilize your skills with their best clients or other industry-related influencers. These relationships are often discovered and deepened through your best clients, and for that reason you should focus initially on developing your best existing relationships.
- Positional relationships are the key and the difference between growing by twenty percent through grunt work or growing by as much as eighty percent or more and having a blast the whole time. These relationships are your top clients and best cheerleaders. Those who fully utilize and appreciate your value and can't help but introduce you to others, such as their accountants, lawyers, peers, family, and friends. Like the example of the cross-disciplinary lunch and learn, these relationships have other advisors, complicated situations, and understand the value of paying for good advice.

Think about it like this. When the phone rings, there are those who you can't wait to talk to, and then there are those who you roll your eyes at. These clients are the former, and your goal is to lead the team of their inner circle to new value while earning new sources of revenue and ultimately new trusted referrals, which we prefer to call "introductions."

So, before you can jump out there and start duplicating your best clients (think about how cool that is in itself!), you need to complete your prep work.

Exercise: Resources – Relationships

Using the following chart as a guide, you can begin to aggregate your households. Take time to account for ALL accounts. (Note that a household may represent multiple accounts (husband, wife, business retirement, and a college fund, for example).

You will be able to determine which clients are ideal for duplicating, and how they can help you do so.

Considerations:

#	Household	Total Accounts	Total Gross Revenue (Rolling 12)	Transactional / First Year Only Fees	Retired / Employed	Business Owner	Recurring Revenue / Investments	Recurring Revenue / Insurance	Recurring Revenue / Planning	Projected (Recurring Rev combined)	Retirement Income Planning	Estate Planning / Tax	Business Succession and Insurance	Health Insurance and Benefits Review	Personal Life and Long-Term Care	Education & Generational Planning	Charitable Planning	Goals Planning	Special Needs Planning	Relationship (Hot/Warm/Cold/None/Self) - Tax	Relationship (Hot/Warm/Cold/None/Self) - Legal	Relationship (Hot/Warm/Cold/None/Self) - Insurance	Relationship (Hot/Warm/Cold/None/Self) - Investment	Relationship (Hot/Warm/Cold/None/Self) - Planning	Relationship (Hot/Warm/Cold/None/Self) - Benefits	Relationship (Hot/Warm/Cold/None/Self) - Banking
1	Mr. and Mrs. Fancy Pants	4	$23,000	$6,300	Emp.	Yes	$10,000	$4,300	$2,500	$16,700	Done	Need	Need	Need	Need	Need	Need	Done	NA	Warm	Self	Self	Self	Self	Self	Cold
2																										
3																										
4																										
5																										

– Continue until all relationships are accounted for.

- How many households do you have?
    o Using the recurring revenue totals, how many households are paying you what you need to make according to your target EPH exercise?
    o How many are you allowing to hold you back?
- How many opportunities do you have to increase your value to your top clients?
    o How many opportunities do you have with existing clients below your target EPH that can be revisited?
    o How many of your clients have generational, estate, or special needs planning you have not yet done that could lead to new relationships?

- o How many business owner clients do you have that could lead to employee benefits and retirement relationships?
- How many of your top relationships have other professionals that you could deepen by driving holistic team meetings?
  - o How many of your smaller transactional clients could benefit from cross-discipline planning and may have the potential to cross over your target EPH?
  - o How many are not likely to ever reach your target EPH and need to manage accordingly (through automated service models, raising fees, or partnering)?

In our private coaching, we address these strategies in more detail. However, just getting a handle on your situation can highlight dozens of opportunities for new services and revenue, and just as many new relationships for duplicating your best clients.

Start now and build a strong foundation through data and organization. Update your profile as you go, and for further help, visit the workbook section of this Quest and update your profile online.

Final Thoughts

"Okay Joe, I said I would keep an open mind I am still question this whole process. What is Q4 exactly and what is this Quest really all about? Are you suggesting I work hard or that I relax and be content with fate?"

"Yes" Joe said with a smile. Now you are starting to see. You see Ron the two are not mutually exclusive. Whatever gifts, skills, resources, and passions you have you should do with all your vigor. You have been furnished a flame for those things in a way that only you can do perfectly in such a proportion. Yet, at the same time the results are to measures in the experience, the love, and the journey, and not in material gain. That is where joy come from!"

"So then how do we quantify or measure that success?"

"That, my brother, is the right question. Let us continue"

Q4

EXPECTATION

Expectation Covers:

- **Precision**
   Exercise: Three Eulogies
- **Pairing**
   Exercise: Self, Service, Stuff
- **Prioritization**
   Exercise: Priority Pathway

Precision

Define Your Success Expectation

The fourth and final step to the Q4 Quest has clearly defined reasonable expectations. If you don't know where you're going, how will you know when you get there? And, if you don't have a map, how will you know if you get off track? This step pulls your life together and prepares for playing to win.

Playing to win

Poet Maya Angelou said, "Success is liking yourself, liking what you do, and liking how you do it." I like that. As my father told me, "Whether you are playing a game of cards, building a business, or raising your own family, the object of the game is winning." But what is winning? It is important to get this right. Is winning a scoreboard or a life well-lived, and what does that mean? What is it for you? Not your boss, your spouse, or anyone, but you.

When we define the rules, nothing and no one can take away our victory but ourselves. For example, look at the little league team, and consider how many different experiences we can have by simply defining success on our own terms.

As a coach starting our inaugural little league season, we decided very early on not to let our team be a place for politics, cranky parents, or nervous children. I suggested we collectively define success. Were we playing to grow together as friends and a team, were we playing to build stronger fundamentals of the sport, or were we playing only to win as much as possible? Maybe we just wanted to have fun? Depending how we collectively answered that question would significantly influence how we executed. Having clarity from the beginning on what mattered most to us in this context lead to an amazing season for all.

So how do YOU define success?

The Vision

"Once, during a consulting session," Papa Joe recalled a vivid client experience.

"I was working with a client through the Q4 process when he told me how these exercises were stimulating him in all-new ways. Q4 had been refocusing on him on pleasant memories, great people, and applying passions he had not considered for a long time. Jeff told me how as he laid in bed at night, he had pleasant thoughts dance around in his brain like a Pink Floyd light show.

"Admittedly, he was hesitant at first to discuss intimate details with me, let alone to embrace planning from such a "mushy" place, as he put it. He had never really been the type to take much time for thinking introspectively or philosophically, so for him, it felt a little strange.

"However, as we proceeded, it came more naturally. My friend recounted how one night, these typically abstract images formed a solid picture. It was a beautiful face. A female face that he recognized.

"'Wow,'" he thought. 'Am I dreaming?' The woman reached out and took his hand, and she whispered, 'Follow me.' Without pause, he did, as she took him gliding gracefully across the floor out into his living room. With his hand held lovingly in hers, they entered the living room. However, he thought, 'Who are all these people? Did I sleep in longer than I thought? Am I am still dreaming?'

"He stood there, half asleep and fully confused. He could not help but see that no one was paying him any mind. Instead, everyone's focus was aimed toward the front of the room, where his favorite recliner was set aside to make way for a podium and a cheap microphone.

"Standing on his toes, he bounced up and down, trying to see past the wall of his friends and family. He could only make out the backs of the people's heads, except for three distinct faces at the front of the room looking back in his direction. One, he recognized immediately as a friend from his childhood. Another moment passed, and he recognized the second as his current partner, but the third person he still could not discern.

"'What is all this?' he asked in a perplexed and slightly annoyed tone as he pushed his way past her to get a better view. Still, all that he could see now was a portable easel off to the side with a picture on it.

"'That is a picture of me!' he shouted as he read the words underneath, which read, 'Welcome to Jeff's Memorial.' He turned around, demanding an explanation, but no one was there. All he saw were the piercing red numbers of his alarm clock staring back at him from the side of his bed. It was all a dream.

"Now, I have often wondered about that story. What would my friends say about me at my funeral? After countless hours daydreaming about Jeff's dream, I concluded the first face represented a friend from his past, the second a current relationship, and the third, I believe, is someone he has yet to meet.

"With this as a backdrop, writing what each of these people might say at our own viewing can really help us to articulate what we really want to be known for. In other words, what is your legacy? How will you be remembered in the world? Did you leave it a better place than when you came into it?"

Exercise: The Three Eulogies

Looking back over this last story, consider each of the three visitors and ask yourself what they might say about you if this was your viewing. Using the following questions as a guide, write your three eulogies.

(1) Past – Who is that one person (you can only pick one) who helped to make you who you are today?
- What kind of person would they say you were? Why did they like you?
- What impact on others or the world would they say your presence made?
- How would they highlight your journey together?
- Be boldly honest here. Why did they work with you? (What did they see in you that you have not seen in yourself?)
- At your memorial, what do you hope they would say about you that captures what made them most proud of you as a person?
- With honest introspection, and based on how you live today, what are those inconsistencies with how they see you and how you truly are?

Complete your "eulogy" exercise here.

(2) Present – Name the person (a peer, close friend, or mentor) who pours energy into you and challenges you to be the best version of yourself.
- What kind of person would they say you are?
- What impact on others or the world would they say your presence makes?

- How would they highlight your journey together?
- Be honest here. Why do they enjoy working with you? (What positive attributes of your character do you think they see in you that you do not yet believe about yourself?)
- At your memorial, what do you hope they would say about you that captures what made them most proud of you as a person?
- With honest introspection, based on how you live today, what are those inconsistencies with how they will come to see you and how you truly are today?

> Write your "present" exercise here.

(3) Future – From someone you have yet to meet (or at least develop a meaningful relationship with), who is the person you believe will challenge you to become a person you would like to work closely with?
- What kind of person do you hope they say you are?
- What impact on others or the world would they say your presence made?
- How would they highlight your journey together?
- Be honest here. Why would they want to work with you? What aspects of your character do you need to work on that might entice them to work with you?
- At your memorial, what do you hope they would say about you that captures what made them most proud of you as a person?
- With honest introspection, based on how you live today, what are those inconsistencies with whom you hope they will see and how you live today?
- What has this exercise revealed to you about where you came from, where you are, and where you might go as a person?
- What inconsistencies might you see in how they see you, and how you see yourself living today?

- What changes might this exercise encourage?

> Write your "future" exercise here.

In our private coaching, we address these strategies in more detail. The time put into self-exploration pays dividends in growth, magnetic marketing, relationship building, and managing reservations.

For further help, visit the workbook section of this Quest and update your profile online.

Pairing

Chasing the Joneses

"Let me ask Ron, have you defined your success, or have you allowed someone else to define it for you?" Joe asked already knowing the answer.

"Consider this. Anyone who has ever bought a new car knows that as you do, you see what you bought everywhere. Why? Because whatever we focus on is what we see. Many people have tried to make changes in their life by focusing on their past experiences and reliving their past mistakes. However, a future of sustainable significance begins by focusing on how you think TODAY! After all, a mile is merely a collection of feet. You have two, so pick one and move it!"

In contrast to this past analysis, as many business plan reviews do too much of, solutions-based counseling focuses on the solutions and potential in front of us. Forward-looking advice is more about taking one incremental and manageable step from where we are in the direction we want to go. It is about simply dropping baggage from the past and not reliving it. It is also about exchanging our anxieties about the future into energies for today.

Many of us have allowed someone else or society to define our success. My kids, for example, are always reporting to me who in their school has a bigger house or a new car, or a great vacation planned. In some ways, we eventually learn there will always be someone with a bigger house, more money, or a faster car, and the end of this train of thought is bleak. Unfortunately, I am not so certain that adults have outgrown "keeping up with the Joneses."

We have all also likely found ourselves looking around comparing ourselves to others from careers, to titles, houses, how our children behave or score in school, or where we go on vacation. Each comparison is an unnecessary weight we place on ourselves. Pressures that ironically rob us of joy. How many external pressures have we taken upon ourselves as our definitions of success? Now, what if we defined success on our own terms?

Exercise: Self, Service, Or Stuff

How do you define success? This might be thought of as your professional "Love Language."

Are you driven by self-actualization and progress (self)? Or perhaps you are most passionate about helping others (service)? Or maybe you chase a certain lifestyle (stuff)?

The reality is you probably are driven by elements of all three, but not probably in equal proportion.

In the spirit of all that we have done so far, take another minute and put a quantifiable measure to what constitutes success in your own life. Now, using the chart below, consider the three areas of self-stuff-service and follow the instructions outlined.

1) Rank them in order of personal preference, with one being the most important, and three being the third in importance. Remember, this is your journey and not the Joneses. If all you want is a fast car today, then say so. Inversely, if you just want to help the homeless regardless of your personal financial situation, then say that. The only wrong answer is a lie.

2) Next – Help to demonstrate how you might categorize these three priorities by using nine chips, spreading them out across each of

the three boxes below. You can spread them evenly or put them all in one box. Just be honest.
3) Lastly, describe a specific goal in the appropriate box. (a specific bucket list trip, or ideal home, or the new Cruiser)

	Self	Stuff	Service
Includes:	Influence / Accolades	Lifestyle	Impact / Legacy
Rank:	1 / 2 / 3	1 / 2 / 3	1 / 2 / 3
Chips: 1-9			
Specific Goals			

In our private coaching, we address these strategies in more detail. The time put into self-exploration pays dividends in growth, magnetic marketing, relationship building, and managing reservations.

For further help, visit the workbook section of this Quest and update your profile online.

Prioritization

One Step at a Time

So, if each journey begins with a specific step. Let's take the first one together. Your mission and your vision should lead the way always lead the way. This is what we call the north star, so it is imperative that you have yours formulated.

Next, think about what your life would like five years from now if everything you dream might have come to fruition. How would you know? What would your life look like? How would your morning start differently? A brisk run on the beach, more time in the Good Book, a bold cup of coffee, or a smile from your favorite person?

Now, think about where your life is today on a scale of one to ten, with one being "needs work" and ten being "perfect". Where do you feel your life is today? What would it take to move your life even a fraction of a number closer to perfect? Say from a six to a 6.5? Write that down.

Looking back at everything we have covered, begin consolidating all your previous goals and exercises, so we can appropriately focus and build the most efficient pathway for your personal Q4 Quest.

To help you, consider using TRAMS goals. The inverse of 'SMART" goals.

These goals are specific, measurable, and relevant to your personal journey and no one else's. For a long time, people asked if the goal was SMART. If you haven't heard of it before, here is a quick summary.

- The "S" stood for specific. This meant to choose a small and well-defined part of the goal. Do not just try to swallow a watermelon.
- The "M" stood for measurable. You, as the user would be able to see the progress of your goal because it would be quantifiable.
- The "A" was attainable, and the purpose was to make sure the goal was realistic in a realistic time frame. Yes, you could plan to run across the United States. It would not be realistic to say you were doing so in two days.
- The "R" was relevant to your goals.
- The "T" was time-based, and you would set a date on the goal.

Overall, this was not a bad strategy for goal setting. However, if you were paying attention to the book, it is a step backward from everything we have been trying to help you understand. The way to follow the Q4 Quest is to set TRAMS goals. Why? So, we end with an action step towards a dream rather than a dream to take action.

Look back over everything we have discussed, especially your motivations and relationship mapping, and begin to lay down your TRAMS goals.

Time-bound
Relevant
Attainable
Measurable
Specific

In our private coaching, we address these strategies in more detail. But for further help, visit the workbook section of this Quest and update your profile online.

Finally, once you have collected all of your relevant goals, we move to the final part of your Quest development—the Priority Pathway. Using the pathway exercise below, you may now bring everything together into a visual workflow and personal journey.

Take time to revisit each exercise and look for inconsistencies in how you have been living and the life you know you were made for. Make a list of necessary actions prioritized from highest to lowest until all changes have been accounted for.

(It may be helpful for some to consider completing one path for your personal life and a separate one for your professional life).

Priority Pathway

Time Bound	
Relevant	
Attainable	
Measurable	
Specific	

Revisiting each of your Q4 Quest exercises, list all of your TRAMS goals here

Now using the following chart begin to segment your goals in terms of proximity.

Priority Pathway

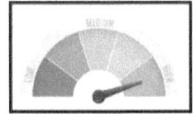

For further help, visit the workbook section of this Quest and update your profile online.

Final Thoughts

"So help me out Joe. We have talked about love, service, relationships, perspective, transformation, passion, hard work, joy, and now redefining success on our own terms. Won't that be hard when everything and everyone around us seems to be using a different plumb line or benchmark?"

"You betcha" chuckled Joe. "I did know you were still trying to be like everyone else?"

"Well sure, but still . . ."

"But nothing brother. Many are called but few are chosen. Are you among the chosen?"

"Here's the thing Ron. If you cannot get there from here in your head then you will never get there until you change your thinking like we discussed in part two. If you can. It get there physically then you need to change or at least better manage your situation like we discussed in section three. If you are still not sure about all this then go back to the beginning and look at the faces of those nearest to your heart and decide who and what matters most to you, really. But, if you have clarity on those basics then define success your way, not anyone else's, and play to win! That my friend is a glorious life and an awesome existence. That my friend will make you a magnetic leader in business and the right people foe you will be drawn to you like a moth to a flame."

Conclusion

Our conclusion is just the beginning of your Quest!

- **Visualizing your goals using the look back test**
  Exercise: Look back test
- **Knowing where to be**
  Exercise: Litmus Test

Coming together

If you're stuck in a rut and burned-out but know you have more inside you, or are simply struggling to break through to the next level, chances are you are playing by the wrong set of rules and lying to yourself about where you are putting your energy. It's not entirely your fault.

Standardized testing in schools, fake-news propaganda, predatory social media, and gorilla marketing are all contributing factors reducing each of us to mere numbers. We are losing the value of real relationships, we are missing a supportive community, and our businesses are reflecting this. Today, long-term lifestyle planning such as retirement or estate planning has unabashedly become a conversation more about dollars than dreams. Couple this now with an inherited business culture consumed far more by gold than the golden rule, and it's no wonder our humanity and our happiness are disappearing along with our passion and purpose. In short, we have all been trained wrong, and we are suffocating.

While society may have contributed to your current shortfalls, it's entirely your fault if you choose to stay stuck living anything less than the best version of yourself. Let sustainable significance and the Q4 process guide you back to the "you" that you know you were made for.

Exercise: Horizon (Or Look Back Test) Test

Finally, we jump onto the journey and start to live a truly Q4 life. Using the Horizon test below, let's make sure we haven't missed the forest for the trees by answering a few engagement questions.

- Five years from now, or even one year from now, if we were to reflect on your life, comparing it to where it is today, what things would you have had to change that would demonstrate the benefit of our journey together?
- Now, on a scale of one to ten (ten being the greatest), rate the following:

  _____ Before we started working on this, how satisfied were you with your path's potential?

  _____ After you have completed this work, how satisfied are you?

  _____ What's the first thing that you will do, or notice from your initial progress?

  _____ What's one thing you can do that will not bump your satisfaction even a fraction today?

Remember to be realistic. This is a marathon, not a sprint. In fact, when we are living authentically the journey is the destination. There is no such thing as 110 percent. In fact, even at one hundred percent, we will inevitably burn out or be forced to give everything only a fraction of our focus and energy, or both.

Following Through

After a sip of now cold coffee Joe resumed, "Remember Ron how important it is to have a vision. A vision without a plan is just a dream, and a plan without accountability isn't worth the paper it's written on. Action is essential for sustainable significance, but can also be dangerous. For example, if you have built a strong business plan, you likely start out excited to dive in. However, you may also come to find that accountability is daunting."

"Right" Ron confirmed enthusiastically.

"Don't beat yourself up over it. Take a deep breath and recognize the blessing that you can go back and reassess. I would be more concerned if you were doing everything perfectly and were still having problems. But how are you managing your accountability? (How might someone else be managing your performance?) Let's look at two ways to manage accountability.

"The common way that most have been taught goes like this. Assesses your progress from point to point in a rear-view mirror condemning any actions that fall short of some arbitrary benchmark, like looking at sales or goals at the end of your quarter or year, and condemning yourself for not meeting them (if that's the case). The other, more positive way is to paint our potential ahead of time and monitor what activities we do and the results they produce,. Then we focus on doing more of what we are doing good at and grow with excitement into our potential.

"For example, most of us are accustomed to the generic business plans that suggest we hit some number annually, break it down quarterly, and then add some arbitrary growth factor of say ten percent. Now, if we hit it, so what, it was kind of made up, anyway. However, if we do not hit the goal, we start working each month, week, and day under the gun. In other words, we've doubled down on the stress without any improvement to our situation. That sounds like a recipe for disaster."

"Are you suggesting we don't have accountability?" questioned Ron.

"Not at all Ron. I am suggesting we lead more with the carrot than the stick. Consider this discourse between a sales manager and a struggling employee I once worked with and see just how absurd rearview accounting is to a Q4 Quest.

"Boss," asked Mark, "have you ever been in a sales slump as long as me?"

"Sure, Mark. Sales is a game of feast or famine. One month, we're high on the mountain, and the next month, we're digging holes in the valley! That's the name of the game."

"So, why are you not cracking whips, boss? My friends at other firms would have gotten chewed out by now."

"That's easy, my friend, if you are in the right business, and I believe that you are, then we're plenty hard enough on ourselves. You won't need a whip; you'll need a cheerleader and high fives!"

Mark perked up a bit because he knew that to be true. What a blessing to be working with someone with such insight.

The manager continued, "If you say you don't care enough to win, there's nothing I can say to change that. But I can motivate you and reward you more when you're winning to help keep you high on the mountain as long as possible. That's what a good manager does. Think about it—when you're down in the valley, do you ever start to doubt yourself, your process, or the product?"

"Sometimes . . . well, most of the time!"

"Now, have you also ever had someone applying additional pressure and turning up the heat to make things happen?"

"Yep," Mark chuckled.

"And how did that help your game?"

"It didn't at all. If anything, it just made me more disappointed in myself, and annoyed at the manager."

"Bingo. So, If I hear you right, in that scenario your sales are down, you're disappointed in yourself, annoyed at the people around you, and full of doubt, to boot! I bet that does wonders for your morale, right? When we look at the traditional paradigm through those lenses, it sounds silly. Yet, so many live with that view; it's what they were taught and what they pass on, but it's garbage, and it is bad leadership.

"Let's stick with the much more positive and effective alternative. Continue to look ahead, not behind. Reward the smallest gains, and do not spend much time obsessing over the losses, and there will be many more losses in life and business than wins. Recognize that every 'no' is simply that much closer to the next yes and keep being you. The right moth will come to your flame, and if not, then it was not meant to be, but at least you didn't put out your flame to live a lie.

"When you find out what you love to do, do it, and do it well. Delegate the rest. Now, fight like a champion to win because it's your life and leave it all on the field every day. This way when you win, you win big, and it feels great because you earned it. When you fall, there are no regrets because you left it all on the field. Simply put, find what you love, give it your all, and track because you must, but enjoy the journey. That is happiness. That is living the dream. That is playing to win, and that is sustainable significance.

"That is happiness. That is living the dream. That is flipping the script! That is playing to win."

Exercise: Quick Litmus Test/Reverse Check-Up

You'd be happy to know that through *The Q4 Quest* online, you are never alone. Likewise, whenever you feel stuck, there is a quick litmus test you can use anytime to test your decisions.

Like checking answers in a math class, you can easily check your decision and your journey with a quick life check-up by simply looking back on your journey in reverse.

Do the decisions you are making today:

- align with your priorities (Expectations)?
- utilize your gifts and resources (Situation)?
- passionately enhance your personal mission and vision for the world (Reservations)?
- and provide and protect the people who matter most to you (Motivations)?

Consider this example,

"Do the decisions you are making today align with your priorities in a way that utilizes your gifts and resources, while passionately enhancing your mission and vision for the world and providing and protecting the people you say matter most?"

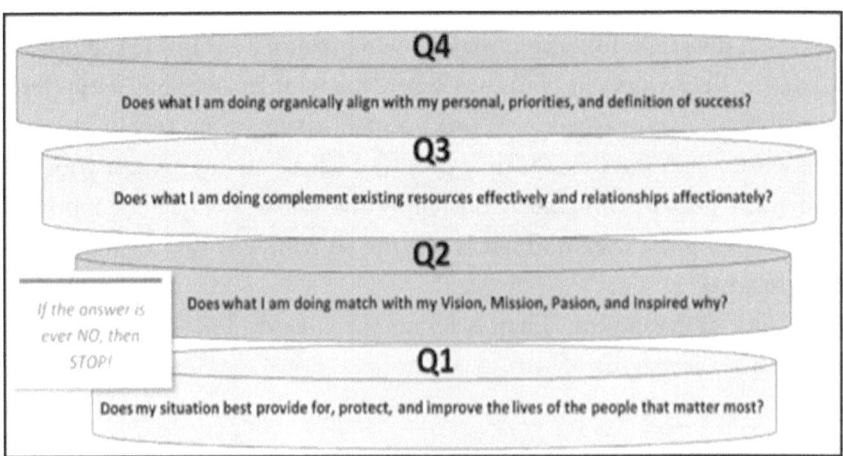

So, when do we start?

Final Thoughts

"Here we are, brother, rock'n the dinner." Joe gestured a toast with his cup.

"Agreed. I think I love this place!" Ron said, smiling over a familiar cup of coffee that had never tasted so good.

Joe knew he had done what he came to accomplish. "I am happy for you, Ron," he said.

With a smile Ron added, "so, break it down for me now, Joe. I get what you're saying. It is simple, but you're also right that it's not easy. I also get that once you see it, you can't unsee it. But I fear after you leave, I might revert back to my old ways."

"Well, you probably will a bit, Ron, but here's the thing. Every time you recognize it, just stop. Turn back to what you have learned through your Quest and don't beat yourself up. It gets easier over time."

"So, can I ask a question, Joe?"

"Of course, what is it?"

"So, what now? I mean, I know you have to move on at some point, but I don't want to lose this . . . whatever this is that we have here."

Joe smiled. "Brother, this is your Quest for Q4, and I have mine."

"Sure, but I still don't know what 'Q4' is?" Ron persisted, making air quotes to emphasize the point.

"Sure you do, Ron."

"No," Ron said with full sincerity, "I don't. What is it?"

With a wink, Joe replied, "You mean 'who' is it." Joe paused to let the truth sink in.

Ron's head tilted like a confused dog for a second to process what he had just heard.

Joe took advantage of the awkward silence to add, "Look around, Ron, just look around.

Ron knew Joe did not just mean to look around the diner but look around at life and everything in it. Everyone in it. Yes. He symbolically scanned the diner in slow orbit, taking in every face and every smile before turning back to his friend. But when he rested his eyes back in Joe's direction, his old friend was gone, just as mysteriously as he had arrived.

All that was left was a napkin with a cross on it and a few words inscribed which read, "Stay true, be kind, and enjoy the ride. I will be with you always. Love Joe."

So, when do we start?

SECTION 2
EXERCISES

INTRODUCTION

Welcome to *The Q4 Quest* workbook, built from a passionate merging of financial services sales practices and psychology for one purpose. Transformation.

Transformation for our communities and businesses through better stewardship.

- *Transformation* for financial clients through sincere and comprehensive relationships.
- *Transformation* for financial professionals like you, your businesses, and your families through actualization.

This journey is the culmination of decades of personal research, experience, and field application. Not to be confused as just another process, Q4 is a transformational way of living your best life, the one you were made for. I hope we will one day all live in a world where sustainably significant self-actualization is not only possible but probable.

Over a few decades, I have had the privilege of seeing the fruits of Q4 change lives in a multitude of settings, from personal pastoral counseling to tens-of-thousands of hours of financial planning for families and corporations, as well as vision casting for businesses, the non-profit sector, and even churches. But maybe most significantly, *The Q4 Quest* is specifically tailored to help financial advisors build amazing businesses and inspiring lives. Are you ready to start your transformational journey?!

How Does It Work?

Like financial planning, Q4 follows a process of uncovering needs and wants, as well as coordination gaps and potential hang-ups. Through a series of field-tested and proven exercises, you will *discover, develop, and deepen* your business potential and your personal success.

As you progress through your journey, you will encounter a series of strategic exercises that build off each other. You will have an opportunity at the beginning of each exercise to assess and gauge your current situation. After each exercise, you can again gauge your progress and comfortability with any new information and prioritize any likely action steps. For example:

"How successful is your process for conditioning your best existing clients for introducing you to their circles of influence?" (Check one)

- ☐ **Low** – I get very few personal introductions from my best clients to their circles of influence each year. I need to work in this area if I want to duplicate my best clients this year.
- ☐ **Medium** – I get a consistent amount of new business through personal introductions but could probably do a bit better if I finetune my process. If I could add a few more top clients next year through existing relationships, it would be worth the time to improve my process.
- ☐ **High** – I got this! I get all the business I can handle through personal introductions. My problem is not in getting new clients, it is in serving them as best possible and I should prioritize my time elsewhere for the time being.

The objective, once all exercises are complete, will be to simply prioritize our time so we can focus on areas that will really "move the needle" first while mitigating other distractions. This clarity makes your Quest clear to "focus on the next most important thing at the time." Period.

Let's move your needle!

Q4 Quest Online

One last thing that makes this Quest so powerful is that this workbook also pairs with our Q4 Quest Online. This is our online, proprietary, interactive personal coaching experience for financial advisors like you. It is like having your own coach or Papa Joe by your side offering wise insight, helpful encouragement, and the occasional necessary accountability.

Imagine knowing the most important things you could be doing daily and having the motivation to do it. Well, you can! Having a virtual coach will provide greater *intrinsic motivation* and a willingness to make new discoveries. According to McKinsey (2018), when employees find greater intrinsic motivation, they are thirty-two percent more committed to their work and forty-six percent more satisfied with their jobs.

Consider these quotes about the importance of having a coach along with your journey:

1. **Discovering the truth** - "A coach is someone who tells you what you don't want to hear, who has you see what you don't want to see, so you can be who you have always known you could be." **Tom Landry – head coach Dallas Cowboys**
2. **Developing your potential** - "I absolutely believe that people, unless coached, never reach their maximum capabilities." **Bob Nardelli – CEO Home Depot**
3. **Deepening your possibilities** - "Coaching is about helping clients unlock the treasure-chest of their lives - worth bearing in mind then that diamonds are made from coal under pressure, and it's the grit in the oyster which creates the pearls." **Sarah Durrant – business coach**
4. **Driving your success** - "Coaching helps you to take responsibility for your life, let go of what others think, and become your true self. It's about you, creating the life that you want - and deserve." **Emma-Louise Elsey – Business Coach and CEO**

If you have not yet set up your online profile, we encourage you to do so now. Your future self will thank you!

Visit us online to set up your free virtual coaching profile!

In ten minutes or less, begin your own personally guided Quest to business success and personal transformation!

When do we start?

Exercise: Preliminary Profile

The first step of this Quest begins here with a preliminary profile. This step may be simple but do not use that as a reason to skip ahead because each step builds on the last, and often the mysteries are missed without context. This is your life, and you owe it to yourself to play to win.

Personal Information			
Name		Relationship Status	
Date of Birth		Partners Date of Birth	
Personal Address		Partners Name	
Personal Phone		Anniversary	
Professional Licenses		Children	
College Degree / Alumni		Unique Information	

Professional Information			
Company Name		Broker / Dealer	
Industry Start Date		Partners Name	
Business Address		Key Employees	
Business Phone		Work Anniversary	
Website		Linked In	
Professional Associations		Facebook	

Community Information		
Social Civic (Lions, Elks, Rotary, etc.)		
Networking Affiliations (BNI, Toastmasters, etc.)		
Professional Associations (CFP, Insurance, etc.)		
Religious involvement		
Non-profit positions		
Specific causes (Cancer, autism, etc.)		

Once you've completed your preliminary profile, update your online Q4 Quest coach and your Q4 Quest Online.

Q1

MOTIVATION

Motivation is a driver - the reason we do what we do! Motivation may be either seen or unseen, and it may come from variables outside of ourselves, or it may be a fire deep within us. At the core, motivation may be understood as the manifestation of our more deep-seated fears and desire.

Motivations

We may desire a healthy marriage, a new home, or maybe a promotion or simply to support a meaningful cause. We may fear being lonely, poor, misunderstood, or sick. But they are really two sides of the same coin. A desire to travel may be stated as a fear of not seeing the world. A desire to be a good provider may be described as the fear of losing financial stability. Even a desire to experience the abundance of life may be expressed as a fear of poor health or even death. So, we start by focusing on the carrot and not the stick.

Exercise: Fear and Desire

Check up from the neck up: Before we begin this exercise, consider the following question. On a scale of one to ten, with one being "not at all" and ten being "all the time", how well do your daily activities align with your most sincere fears and desires? (circle one)

[1 - 2 - 3 - 4 - 5 - 6 - 7 - 8 - 9 - 10]

Exercise: Using the following picture as a guide, fill in the following assessment.

Exercise part (a) Fears:

If this is your workbook, use the space below or login to your Q4 Quest Online. Alternatively, design the exercise yourself by writing "fears" in one column, with a space across from this to respond to this under the heading "what if this were to happen?"

Begin by thinking about your fears; write down the top one or two, and then ask yourself, "If this were to occur, what is the worst that could happen?" Think about a few key fears you might have in business and life and write them down. If you're unsure, examine the previous illustration or revisit *The Q4 Quest* chapter.

Repeat: what else, what else, what else . . . until you have identified the absolute worst thing that could happen in your mind or exhausted your possibilities. It usually takes half a dozen or so scary layers to exhaust our fears well.

Fears	What if this were to happen?

Now, what if instead of focusing on the Fear, you instead focus on the inverse—its Desire.

Using the following chart, restate each fear as a desire, as in the illustration. For example, anxiety became clarity and loss became security. What would your fears become, and what would life be like if all your fears were desires?

(Add any desires that you may not have seen as a fear previously such as the desire to obtain a certain level of wealth, or to provide for a certain lifestyle for your family. Also, add these to exercise part (a) as a restated fear. What might happen if this fear were to come to fruition? Is it worth protecting against, and if so, how are you?)

What if those fears	*Become*	Desires	What would that look like?

Check up from the neck up: After completing this exercise, consider the following question. On a scale of one to ten, with one being "not at all" and ten being "I got it perfectly", how well are your daily activities moving you closer to your desires while protecting you from your fears? (circle one)

[1 - 2 - 3 - 4 - 5 - 6 - 7 - 8 - 9 - 10]

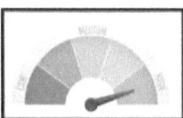

How well aligned are your actions to your personal goals and desires, including providing for and protecting the people you care about? (check one)

- ☐ **Low** – I need help vision casting and prioritizing my daily activities. Likewise, I could use help better protecting my lifestyle and my business from contingencies (market set back, loss of a top client, disability, premature death, etc.)
- ☐ **Medium** – I could use some help to prioritize my action steps to my desires. Likewise, there are some areas where I could better protect my lifestyle and my business from contingencies (market set back, loss of a top client, disability, premature death, etc.)
- ☐ **High** – My goals are being appropriately privatized. Likewise, I have adequately protected my lifestyle and my business from contingencies (market set back, loss of a top client, disability, premature death, etc.)

The objective, once all exercises are complete, will be to simply prioritize our time so we may focus on areas that will really "move the needle" first while mitigating other distractions. This clarity makes your Quest clear: "focus on the next most important thing at the time." Period.

Exercise: Who Matters Most

Have you ever thought about the number of people you actually know? The next exercise goes through multiple levels of relationships. We do this to organize the potential impact these relationships have on your business. This next exercise is a two-part process. First, we will prime you to look at the relationships you have. Then we will write them down to organize these relationships to drive your business and move the needle.

The first part looks like the image below. Start with your immediate circle and fill in what that looks like. These people are usually the main drivers in your life and have a lot of sway in your decision making. These are the individuals in your tribe who help make your mission a reality. The next circle deals with strong influencers to help keep you aligned in your vision and are beacons in your life to tell you if you're headed in the right direction.

Check up from the neck up: Before we begin this exercise, consider the following question. On a scale of one to ten, with one being "not at all" and ten being "I got it perfectly", how well are your current relationships included in your business and life planning? (circle one)

[1 - 2 - 3 - 4 - 5 - 6 - 7 - 8 - 9 - 10]

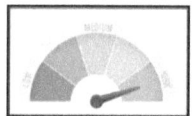

Exercise part 1.

Using the following chart, prime your brain for the upcoming relationship mapping exercise. Laid out below are the six tiers of our personal relationships. Now, think about how each one affects your story.

(1) Six-tier relationship model
  1. **Family** – Family members and their significant relations (parents, spouses, in-laws, children, grandchildren, nieces, nephews, etc.).

2. **Friends** and extended circle of Influence – Close friends, neighbors, and others of personal significance such as business partners or key employees that are like family.
3. **Those You Serve** – Those who you are uniquely qualified and compelled to serve in business and life such as clients, community causes, or social and political agendas.
4. **Those You Serve with** – Meaningful peers or colleagues such as business relationships, partners, key advisors, coaches, or family members.
5. **Champions** – Key mentors and outspoken advocates who might be instrumental in your life and/or mission.
6. **Challengers** – Difficult (business or personal) relationships that may prevent happiness or growth in any area.

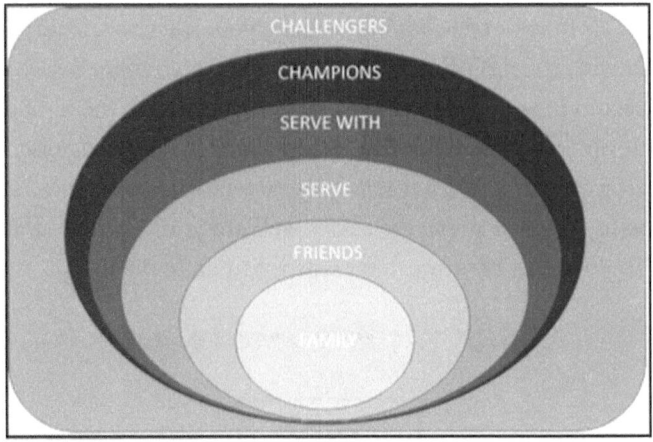

Now how do we use this?

Exercise Part 2

(2) Relationship Mapping
   Next, expand on the previous list using the relationship mapping model depicted below.

Using a bulletin board, whiteboard, or legal pad, map your previously listed relationships and any pertinent details. (Of all the tools I have ever seen, the most effective for purposeful planning by far is "relationship mapping").

Relationship mapping helps to first visualize each of your previously collected relationships in terms of proximity and impact. Second, it makes it easy to see where decisions made might influence (or be influenced by) the people around us.

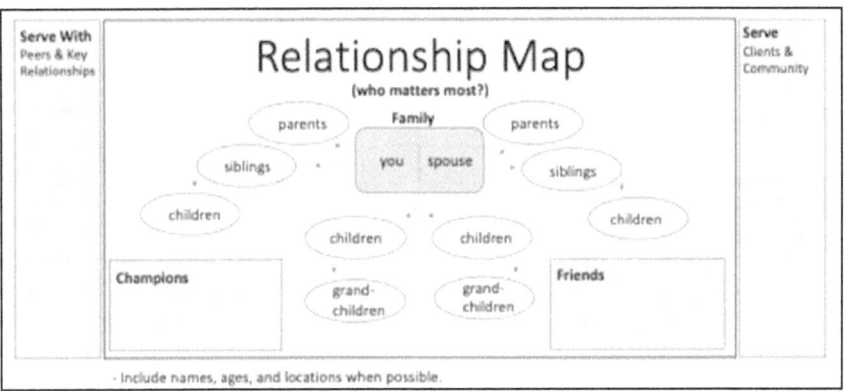

Additional Provoking Question(s): Try to answer before reading on.

- If you could design the perfect dinner with anyone living today, who would it be and why? (Was it your spouse or family member? What does your answer tell you about yourself?)
- If there's someone in your life you must interact with, but they also rub you the wrong way, how do you deal with the situation and why? (Does your solution seek improvement by attempting to change someone else or by changing something about yourself? What does your answer tell you about yourself?)

Family			
	You	name / age	
	Spouse	name / age	
	Children	name(s) / age(s)	name(s) / age(s)
	Children	name(s) / age(s)	name(s) / age(s)
	Children	name(s) / age(s)	name(s) / age(s)
	Other	name(s) / age(s)	name(s) / age(s)

Friends / peers			
Key relationships	name / role		name / role
Key relationships	name / role		name / role
Key relationships	name / role		name / role
Those you serve			
Ideal client type(s)	name / describe		name / describe
Ideal client type(s)	name / describe		name / describe
Ideal client type(s)	name / describe		name / describe
Specific causes	name / describe		name / describe
Those you serve with			
Colleagues, partners, coaches	name / describe		name / describe
Colleagues, partners, coaches	name / describe		name / describe
Colleagues, partners, coaches	name / describe		name / describe
Colleagues, partners, coaches	name / describe		name / describe
Champions			
Mentors, advocates, alliances	name / describe		name / describe
Mentors, advocates, alliances	name / describe		name / describe
Mentors, advocates, alliances	name / describe		name / describe
Key referral sources (KRCs)	name / describe		name / describe
Key referral sources (KRCs)	name / describe		name / describe
Key referral sources (KRCs)	name / describe		name / describe

After you've worked through this exercise, reflect on your circle's layout. These people are the ones that take you on the pathway to your Q4 Quest. The more you put into these exercises, the easier your path can become. Make sure you update your Q4 Quest Online and keep yourself accountable in the revolution of your life.

Check up from the neck up: After completing this exercise, consider the following question. On a scale of one to ten, with one being "not at all" and ten being "I got it perfectly", how well are you currently leveraging your existing relationships to improve your business and your life? (check one)

[1 – 2 – 3 – 4 – 5 – 6 – 7 – 8 – 9 – 10]

How well does your current plan include, provide for, and protect the key relationships in your business and life?

- ☐ **Low** – My current planning needs work, and I tend not to leverage my relationships very well. I would like to look for ways to get more out of the relationships I already have.
- ☐ **Medium** – My current business has and utilizes some key relationships, but could get better. Having a formal process for engaging and motivating key relationships could help my business go to the next level!
- ☐ **High** – I am comfortable with my relationships and systematically manage both personal and business relationships effectively. Training others to help grow and sustain my processes is the likely next step.

Remember, once all exercises are complete the objective is to prioritize our time so we focus on areas that will really "move the needle" first while mitigating other distractions. This clarity makes your Quest clear: "focus on the next most important thing at the time." Period.

Exercise: Personal Vision Statement

According to Forbes (2019), a well-crafted personal vision statement can help avoid detours, provide inspiration to drive your thinking forward, give a clearly defined roadmap, and elevate you from being average. The best business leaders generally have them, so why shouldn't you?

Below we will create the steps to forge your own north star. Take your time in this step as it will help guide future exercises by helping you align the choices you make to keep you on your path.

Check up from the neck up: Before we begin this exercise, consider the following question. On a scale of one to ten, with one being "not at all" and ten being "I got it perfectly", how well do you feel that personal vision statement is accurate of your "best life." (circle one)

[1 - 2 - 3 - 4 - 5 - 6 - 7 - 8 - 9 - 10]

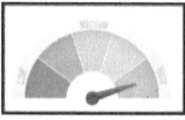

To get you primed for this exercise, let's review the parts of a vision statement:

- **Your dream** – Capture how you see your life's work impacting the world or the community (like the Martin Luther King speech "I have a dream")—Vision Statement.
- **Your part** – To help transition to your mission statement, capture in your journal what contribution your gifts add to that vision.
- **Your tagline** (Bumper Sticker) – To help make it memorable, capture in your journal your life's bumper sticker that reflects the essence of your vision.

Start with your dream. Your work mostly deals with the safety and security of other's lives. How could you capture that in your own words?

Next, you should process what influence you can have on your dream. What special trait do you have that can make the dream to reality?

Your tagline should be a fun stamp of who you are for this quest. Through some introspective questions, you should be able to draw out a conclusive quip.

Finally, put all those sentences together. Then chop out the unessential items to make your personal vision statement one to two sentences.

Now you have a crafted personal vision statement, step back and look at it. Does this capture the change you wish to see in the world? Are you excited about it? How would you feel showing this to your friends?

If you've wavered on any of these questions, go back up and change the responses. If you feel solid about it, remember to update your Q4 Quest Online to continue along with your Q4 Quest.

Check from the neck up: After completing this exercise, consider the following question. On a scale of one to ten, with one being "not at all" and ten being "I have a perfect personal vision statement", how well does your personal vision statement keep you pointed towards your north star?

[1 - 2 - 3 - 4 - 5 - 6 - 7 - 8 - 9 - 10]

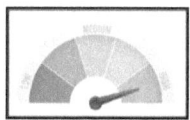

How well does your personal vision statement attract the customers your business deserves? (check one)

- ☐ **Low** – I do not have a vision statement or at least nothing that accurately reflects how I see "my world" and those I serve better because of my work. I could benefit from crafting a "tattoo worthy" vision statement.
- ☐ **Medium** – My personal vision statement is accurate but is not "tattoo worthy!" I could benefit from fine tuning my skills, my passion, and my purpose to inspire the community I serve.
- ☐ **High** – My vision statement motivates me and those I serve, and I look at it every day! The best thing I could do is to make sure more people know my vision.

Remember, the objective, once all exercises are complete, will be to simply prioritize our time so we may focus on areas that will really "move the needle" first while mitigating other distractions. This clarity makes your Quest clear: "focus on the next most important thing at the time." Period.

Exercise: Personal Mission Statement

Next, take a closer look at your current mission statement. Does it motivate you still? Do you still look at it regularly? Is it more than just a canned text bumper sticker to you? How about your clients? Does it provide a clear pathway towards your goals?

When we look back to the book, we remember that the mission statement describes the details of your vision. It is the way the world or the world you serve is better because of the work you do for it. In the end, your mission statement is YOUR conduit for making wise decisions.

Check up from the neck up: Before we begin this exercise, consider the following question. On a scale of one to ten, with one being "not at all" and ten being "I got it perfect", how well does your personal mission statement capture the essence of your work in a way that inspires you and others? (circle one)

[1 - 2 - 3 - 4 - 5 - 6 - 7 - 8 - 9 - 10]

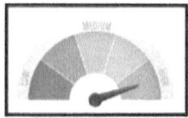

To get ready for this exercise, let's refer back to the book:

- **Who are you compelled to serve?** Write a sentence or two about who you feel you are best equipped to serve, and how.
- **What are you gifted or called to do?**
- **How, or in what way, do you help others?**

Starting with whom you want to serve, did something drive you to get where you are now? Who are the best group of people you can give your skill set to now?

Next, what is your skill set? What unique qualifications do you have to give to the group you want to serve?

What is the unique process you give to your selected community? What is the high-level view of how you do what you do?

Now, put all the sentences you wrote together in a way that makes sense. Your goal is to write out principals and goals that electrify your journey.

Check up from the neck up: After completing this exercise, consider the following question. On a scale of one to ten, with one being "not at all" and ten being "I have a perfect personal mission statement", how well do you feel your personal mission statement lays out the process of your work suited uniquely to those you serve?

[1 - 2 - 3 - 4 - 5 - 6 - 7 - 8 - 9 - 10]

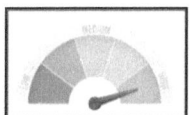

How well do you think your personal mission statement will show to your customers your business can uniquely service their needs? (check one)

- ☐ **Low** – I do not have a mission statement, or at least nothing that accurately reflects how my work improves the lives of those I am called to serve. I could benefit from crafting a unique mission statement that accurately sets me apart from my peers.
- ☐ **Medium** – My personal mission statement is accurate but is not very magnetic. I could benefit from fine tuning my statement to better attract and motivate the community I serve.
- ☐ **High** – My mission statement is unique, motivating, and magnetic, and I look at it every day! The best thing I could do is make sure more people know how to share my mission with the people they care most about.

Again, the objective, once all exercises are complete, will be to simply prioritize our time so we may focus on areas that will really "move the needle" first while mitigating other distractions. This clarity makes your Quest clear: "focus on the next most important thing at the time." Period.

Q1 – Conclusion

Most of us are accustomed to the generic business plans that suggest we hit some number annually, break it down quarterly, and then add some arbitrary growth factor of say ten percent. Now, if we hit it, so what? It was kind of made up, anyway.

Assesses your progress from point to point in a rear-view mirror, condemning any actions that fall short of some arbitrary benchmark, like looking at sales or goals at the end and condemning yourself for not meeting them. The other, more positive way is to paint our potential ahead, monitor what activities we do and the results they produce, and work to do more of what we are good at so we can grow into our potential.

This is the time to pull all the data together. Moving to the last exercise of this section of the workbook, remember you are creating your Q4 Quest. Make sure you feel good moving forward.

Conclusion

Every journey begins with an inch. Left or right is your choice. But pick one and move it! It's time to look back up. Your mission and your vision should lead the way. This is what we call the north star. To get you moving in the right direction, or just moving at all, we ask you to start your Q4 Quest today. What would be the first step?

Revisit each exercise and look for inconsistencies in how you have been living and the life you know you were made for.

Prioritization

In the section "Motivation," we worked through four exercises. Looking back at each of those exercises, consolidate your rankings below.

"Quest-o-meter"

	Low	Medium	High
Fear and Desire			
Relationship Mapping			
Personal Vision Statement			
Personal Mission Statement			

Check up from the neck up: On a scale of one to ten, with one being "needs work" and ten being "near perfect", how complete and compelling was your business and life's foundational motivation aspect of your planning BEFORE doing any of this work?

[1 - 2 - 3 - 4 - 5 - 6 - 7 - 8 - 9 - 10]

Now using that same scale, how complete and compelling is your business BECOMING in response to this foundational work?

[1 - 2 - 3 - 4 - 5 - 6 - 7 - 8 - 9 - 10]

Now, what would it take to move your business even a fraction of a number closer to perfect? (Say from a six to a 6.5?)

So, when do we start?

Horizon (Or Look Back Test) Test

Finally, we jump onto the journey and start to live a truly Q4 life. Using the Horizon test below, let us make sure we haven't missed the forest for the trees by answering a few engagement questions.

- Five years from now, or even one year from now, if we were to reflect on your life, comparing it to where it is today, what things would you have had to change that would demonstrate the benefit of embarking on this quest.
  - Now, on a scale of one to ten (ten being the greatest) rate the following:
  - _____ Before we started working on this quest how satisfied were you with your path's potential?
  - _____ After you have completed this part of the quest how satisfied are you?
  - _____ What's the first thing you will, or do, notice from your initial progress?
  - _____ What's one thing can you do not to bump your satisfaction for even a fraction of a percent today?

Remember to be realistic. This is a marathon, not a sprint. In fact, when we are living, the journey is the destination. There is no such thing as 110 percent. In fact, even at one hundred percent, we will inevitably burn out or be forced to give everything only a fraction of our focus and energy, or both.

Exercise: Quick Litmus Test/Reverse Check-Up

Like checking answers in a math class, you can easily check your decision and your journey with a quick life check-up by simply looking back on your journey in reverse.

Ask yourself, do the decisions you are making today:

- align with your priorities (Expectations)
- utilize your gifts and resources (Situation),
- passionately enhance your personal mission and vision for the world (Reservations),
- and provide and protect the people who matter most to you (Motivations)?

"Do the decisions you are making today align with your priorities in a way that utilizes your gifts and resources, while passionately enhancing your mission and vision for the world and providing and protecting the people you say matter most?"

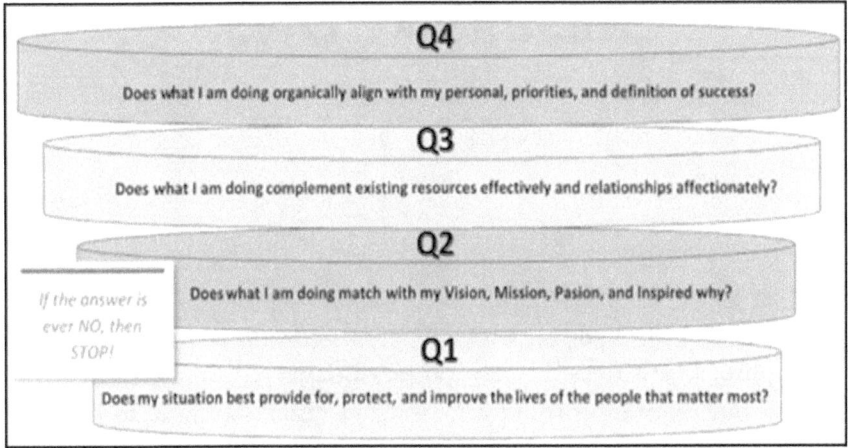

So, when do we start?

Q2

RESERVATIONS

Reservations are the lies that blind us, the baggage we carry, the bad instruction we have received, and the biases we believe.

The desire to change is simple to say, but lasting change is hard to accomplish. But it does not have to be difficult. Changing our actions without our motivation is like a New Year's resolution to go to the gym that lasts ninety days at best.

However, it can be as simple as changing our minds. In other words, personal integrity. Being honest with ourselves about what 'we' want not what we do to please or impress others. Inner peace only requires us to be honest with ourselves about what truly motivates us with a clear picture of who you are, what you care about, and clearly aligned personal vision and mission.

So, to move ahead, recognize that these reservations have been instilled in most of us through not only experience but also education and training. We must rewrite the script and let go of the lies we hold so dear if we want something more than we have today. After all, what we are doing now is getting us what we have now, but you know you have more potential in the tank.

Exercise: Pain

Check up from the neck up: Before we begin this exercise, consider the following question. On a scale of one to ten, with one being "not at all"

and ten being "perfect", how effective are you at recognizing and managing where experiences are shaping and possibly hindering your current decision making? (circle one)

[1 - 2 - 3 - 4 - 5 - 6 - 7 - 8 - 9 - 10]

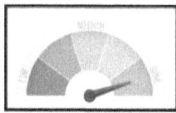

Exercise:

Following the format of *The Q4 Quest* book, take a moment to consider your past. Have you had moments of change resistance? Remember, you have a choice between the pain of change and the pain of not changing. But only one will get you closer to who you know you can be. So, what side of that equation are you on?

Choose words from the list below that describe how you deal when addressing the pains associated with change.

Evasion	prevention	restraint	circumvention
Delay	departure	dodge	dodging
Elusion	escape	escapism	flight
Forbearance	parry	recession	recoil
Retreat	shirking	shunning	abstention
Eschewal	passive resistance	run-around	steering clear of

Of the words you chose, rank them from the least to the most accurate.

1. _____
2. _____
3. _____

Considering now what you have learned through the quest about how we work better with positive reinforcers, write the inverse to the words you selected above?

1. _____
2. _____
3. _____

Food for thought. How might your motivation improve by focusing on your three positive motivators?

Of the words you chose, rank them from the least to the most accurate.

1. _____
2. _____
3. _____

Considering now what you have learned through the quest about how we work better with positive reinforcers, write the inverse to the words you selected above?

1. _____
2. _____
3. _____

Food for thought. How might your motivation improve by focusing on your three positive motivators?

Check up from the neck up: After completing this exercise, consider the following question. On a scale of one to ten, with one being "not at all" and ten being "perfect", how well do you handle the fact past conceptions may need to change? (circle one)

[1 - 2 - 3 - 4 - 5 - 6 - 7 - 8 - 9 - 10]

The Q4 Quest for Financial Advisors

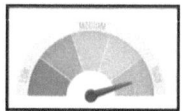

Transformation begins by renewing your mind. How well can you push through the initial stance to renew your mind and transform your life? (check one)

- ☐ **Low** – I do not think I have much in the way of bias or baggage to rethink. I am good the way I am and see little pain to deal with.
- ☐ **Medium** – I am ready for change and recognize I might have some bad habits to break or change, but I have mostly accepted my strengths and weaknesses as they are.
- ☐ **High** – I am hungry for more, and tired of being less than I am capable of for my sake and for those I care about. I WILL push through any initial resistance in my mind, so I can grow out of the pain of not being all I know I can be.

Once all the exercises are complete, we will consolidate them to form a mirror and a reminder of who we could be and how we get in our own way.

Like your car's speedometer reminds us of how fast we are going, The Q4 Quest reminds us to focus what truly maters to us to so we can really move the needle in your business and in life.

Exercise: Partiality

After the excitement of new ideas and new potential fades, it is not unusual to become restless, aggravated, angry, frustrated, or depressed. These feelings are normal, but you must be aware of them to release them.

Check up from the neck up: Before we begin this exercise, consider the following question. On a scale of one to ten, with one being "not at all" and ten being "perfect", how well have your biases mitigated, so you accept new information and new ways to build your business and your life? (circle one)

[1 - 2 - 3 - 4 - 5 - 6 - 7 - 8 - 9 - 10]

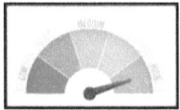

Exercise:

Following Papa Joe through the Q4 Quest, we come to Partiality. Partiality must deal with life after the initial realization that change is needed wears off so that we don't fall back into our old ways.

Choose words from the list below that resonate with you when you think of bias and partiality.

Bigotry	favoritism	inclination	intolerance
Leaning	preference	prejudice	tendency
Tilt	unfairness	bent	chauvinism
Disposition	flash	proclivity	illiberality
mind-set	penchant	preconception	predilection

Of the words you chose, rank them in order from the least to most accurate.

1. _____
2. _____
3. _____

Considering the quest will work better with more positive reinforcers, write of the inverse of the words you most connected with?

1. _____

2. _____
3. _____

How might your motivation improve by focusing on your three personal motivators? Check up from the neck up: After completing this exercise, consider the following question. On a scale of one to ten, with one being "not at all" and ten being "perfect", do you feel your partiality is flexible enough to allow new ideas that will influence your Q4 Quest? (circle one)

[1 - 2 - 3 - 4 - 5 - 6 - 7 - 8 - 9 - 10]

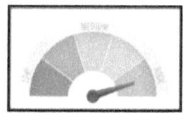

Describe how well you think your partiality is under control enough to accept new ideas to transform your life? (Check one)

- ☐ **Low** – I am not likely to change at this stage in the game.
- ☐ **Medium** – I am open to change, but I know I move slowly even when it's in my best interest.
- ☐ **High** – I get it. If I want to see new results, I need new ways to see and do things. I am open-minded and committed.

Once all the exercises are complete, we will consolidate them to form a mirror and a reminder of who we could be and how we get in our own way.

At times we all need a reminder to refocus our minds on things that truly matter, and this will help you keep "moving the needle" in your business and your life.

Exercise: Pride Reservations

When it comes to pride, we really must be careful. It's understandable to be proud of something you've accomplished. In the context of being too proud to change, however, pride can be one of the biggest roadblocks along your pathway. You may know something is wrong or desire to change, but blinded by pride you find yourself doing everything but the work that is necessary. Buying new programs, investing in new marketing, or attending a conference, but when the dust settles, you have little more to show for your actions but another bill.

If you find yourself saying things like, "I've always done it this way," or I never had to do this before, and I am successful" then rest assured, pride will keep you on the path to nowhere new.

Check up from the neck up: Before we begin this exercise, consider the following question. On a scale of one to ten, with one being "not at all" and ten being "perfect", how well have your biases been mitigated so you accept new information and ways to build your business and your life? (circle one)

[1 - 2 - 3 - 4 - 5 - 6 - 7 - 8 - 9 - 10]

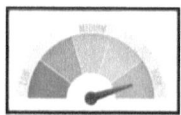

Exercise

In this exercise you will again pick a word from a list. The words you're trying to search for are moments you failed at something and refused to change. In retrospect, what words resonate with you?

The Q4 Quest for Financial Advisors

Choose from the list below:

Disdain	*assumption*	*cockiness*	*conceit*
Condescension	*contumely*	*disdainfulness*	*egoism*
Egotism	*haughtiness*	*hauteur*	*hubris*
immodesty	*insolence*	*loftiness*	*Narcissism*
overconfidence	*patronage*	*pragmatism*	*pretentiousness*

Of the words you chose, rank them from the least to most accurate.

1. _____
2. _____
3. _____

Considering the quest will work better with more positive reinforcers, what is the opposite of the words you most connected with?

1. _____
2. _____
3. _____

How might your motivation improve by focusing on your three positive motivators?

Check up from the neck up: After completing this exercise, consider the following question. On a scale of one to ten, with one being "not aware" and ten being "perfectly aware" of how pride can blind us of our faults and limit our potential, how do you see your own self-awareness? (circle one)

[1 - 2 - 3 - 4 - 5 - 6 - 7 - 8 - 9 - 10]

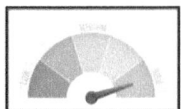

How well can you manage your pride to open paths to new potential? (Check one)

- ☐ **Low** – I do not think there is such a thing as being too proud. I call it confidential and do not want to change in this area of my life.
- ☐ **Medium** – At times, I can become egotistical and know if I were humbler, it would make me more approachable. I am ready to work on managing my pride for the sake of bettering my business and my life.
- ☐ **High** – I can leave my ego at the door. I have thick skin and I am on fire, so bring it on!

Again, once all the exercises are complete, we will consolidate them to form a mirror and a reminder of who we could be and how we get in our own way.

At times we all need a reminder to refocus our minds on things that truly matter, and this will help you keep "moving the needle" in your business and your life.

Exercise: Get It Out of Your Head

Now pull it all together. First, take a moment to reflect. In considering this section from the book, what reservations, biases, and other thoughts did you uncover? What might you hold on to that may prevent you from being all that you know you can be?

Take a second to consolidate your reservations here.

(List both the previous perspectives and the new, more positive focus).

	Pain		Partiality		Pride	
	Previous Focus	Positive Focus	Previous Focus	Positive Focus	Previous Focus	Positive Focus
1						
2						
3						

Conclude this exercise by considering the following.

- Write down any thoughts, behaviors, or chatter in your head and put it on paper.
- When you start to stagnate, revisit this exercise, and see if you are repeating past prohibitions of your mind? **STOP!** if you recognize new red flags (as legitimate as they may seem). Add them to the list.

Write your "Reservation" journal here

Whenever the choice you face hits any of the pain points, you should stop. Refocus on your Q4 Quest and make sure your choices are driving your mission. This can help you stay aligned with your vision. Overall, these words can help you build a significantly sustainable life by keeping you in check with what is most important.

Check up from the neck up: After completing this exercise, consider the following question. On a scale of one to ten, with one being "not aware" and ten being "perfectly aware" of how pride can blind us of our faults and limit our potential, how do you see your own self-awareness? (circle one)

[1 - 2 - 3 - 4 - 5 - 6 - 7 - 8 - 9 - 10]

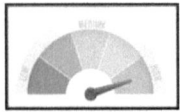

Looking back at your pain, partiality, and pride, how likely are you to commit yourself and your potential?

- ☐ **Low** – I am not into all this introspection stuff. I just want to work hard and let things play out as they will.
- ☐ **Medium** – I am open to new ideas, and I understand the need for being more aware, but it seems odd to build this into my daily practice and my business planning.
- ☐ **High** – I get it. The more we know about ourselves, the better we can walk our authentic life. Our business grows as we do more of what we were made to do and inhibited less by the lies the world would have us believe. I am all in!

Remember, we all need a reminder to refocus our minds on things that truly matter. Now, with these consolidated reservations, start navigating your quest in a way that best helps you to "move the needle" in your business and your life.

Q2 – Conclusion

When we look at the mirror, we feel the immediate urge to judge, criticize, and equate. But we need not fall into this trap. It can defeat the most powerful of people who endure (heroes). Allow yourself the chance to follow your Q4 Quest by turning your downfalls into inspirations.

Prioritization

In the section Reservations, we worked through three areas: pain, partiality, and pride. Now looking back at each of those exercises, consolidate your rankings below.

"Quest-o-meter"

	Low	Medium	High
Pain			
Partiality			
Pride			

Check up from the neck up: On a scale of one to ten, with one being "needs work" and ten being "near perfect", how complete and compelling was your pain, partiality, and pride hampering your progress BEFORE doing any of this work?

[1 - 2 - 3 - 4 - 5 - 6 - 7 - 8 - 9 - 10]

Now using that same scale, how complete and compelling is your pain, partiality, and pride empowering your PROGRESS as a response to this foundational work?

[1 - 2 - 3 - 4 - 5 - 6 - 7 - 8 - 9 - 10]

Now, what would it take to move your business even a fraction of a number closer to perfect? (Say from a six to a 6.5?)

So, when do we start?

Horizon (Or Look Back Test) Test

Finally, we jump onto the journey and start to live a truly Q4 life. Using the Horizon test below, let us make sure we haven't missed the forest for the trees by answering a few engagement questions.

- Five years from now, or even one year from now, if you were to reflect on your life, comparing it to where it is today, what things would you have changed that would demonstrate the benefit of our journey together?
- Now, on a scale of one to ten (ten being the greatest), rate the following:
  - ➤ _____ Before we started working on this, how satisfied were you with your path's potential?
  - ➤ _____ After you have completed this work, how satisfied are you?
  - ➤ _____ What's the first thing that you do or notice from your initial progress?
  - ➤ _____ What one thing can you do not to bump your satisfaction for even a fraction of a percent today?

Remember to be realistic. This is a marathon, not a sprint. In fact, when we are living, the journey is the destination. There is no such thing as 110 percent. In fact, even at one hundred percent we will inevitably burn out or be forced to give everything only a fraction of our focus and energy, or both.

Exercise: Quick Litmus Test/Reverse Check-Up

Like checking answers in a math class, you can easily check your decision and your journey with a quick life check-up by simply looking back on your journey in reverse.

Check if the decisions you are making today:

- Align with your priorities (Expectations)
- Utilize your gifts and resources (Situation),

- Passionately enhance your personal mission and vision for the world (Reservations),
- and provide and protect the people who matter most to you (Motivations)?"

"Do the decisions you are making today align with your priorities in a way that utilizes your gifts and resources, while passionately enhancing your mission and vision for the world and providing and protecting the people you say matter most?"

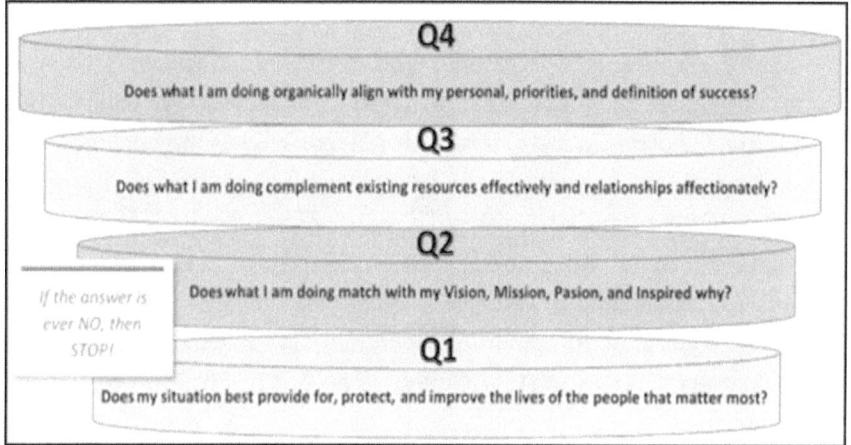

So, when do we start?

Q3

SITUATION

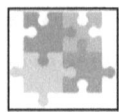

Now for a little less philosophy and a little more action. This next section, situation, may be thought of like the nuts and bolts of your Quest.

Unlike the previous sections, this third section is less introspection and more about personal assessment and inventory. This part of your journey will take you through what we call the 4Ps of your situation: Passions, Personality, Personal Story, and Professional Inventory. Then we will start formulation of the map towards your Q4.

Think about how you can implement these action items into your daily habits. Remember, this is YOUR quest so do not be afraid to be honest, open, and free.

Passion

In life, we can choose to do what everyone around us thinks is best, or we can choose to do what we know we were made to do. It is not until we give ourselves permission to fly our flag and march to our own drum do we find the space to soar. This next exercise is about finding the liberty within ourselves to unapologetically be everything we desire.

Exercise: Passion Assessment

Following the format of *The Q4 Quest* book, consider the following short exercise regarding your passions and gifts. How might you be utilizing or not utilizing your ornate giftedness?

Check up from the neck up: Before continuing with this exercise, consider the following question. On a scale of one to ten, with one being "not at all" and ten being "perfectly aligned", how well do you consider your passions in your career planning?

[1 - 2 - 3 - 4 - 5 - 6 - 7 - 8 - 9 - 10]

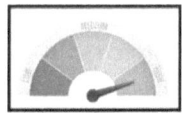

Now using the following three areas, goosebumps, jump-ups, and fun-times, take some time to list keywords that best capture the essence of what makes you excited.

Use the following descriptions to help you fill in the subsequent box.

1. **Goosebumps**: These are those endeavors that give you metaphorical goosebumps, such as surfing or playing drums. *Write three to five words describing these in the box that follows.*
2. **Jump Ups**: These are activities or aspects of your life that excite you and get you jumping out of bed in the morning, such as helping other surfers reach their potential. *Write three to five words describing these in the box that follows.*
3. **Fun times and Hobbies**: Here you might list skills/hobbies that come naturally, and the ones you enjoy. *Write three to five words describing these in the box that follows.*

Goosebumps	Jump-ups	Fun times / hobbies

(Bonus) Additional personal considerations.

- Looking at these questions, what things have you let go of you wish you were still doing?
- In what ways can you reframe your game to include more of your gifts and passions?
- Look at the significance your past can play on your present and future.

Check up from the neck up: After completing this exercise, consider the following question. On a scale of one to ten, with one being "not at all" and ten being "perfectly", how well do your normal daily responsibilities align with the activities you are passionately on fire for?

[1 - 2 - 3 - 4 - 5 - 6 - 7 - 8 - 9 - 10]

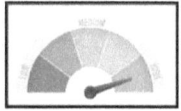

Figuring out how to get up and get on your path is difficult. Are you willing to commit to the motivation you wrote out yourself? (check one box)

- ☐ **Low** – I have fallen into the trap of working now to hopefully one day earn the time and/or money to enjoy life. I could use help to realign my daily responsibilities with the things that most excite me.
- ☐ **Medium** – I enjoy what I do for the most part, and I am passionate about my work. However, I do have additional hobbies that I

could probably find ways to connect with my career that may take my enthusiasm to new heights. I am hungry to explore more possibilities.
- ☐ **High** – I am already living the dream and utilize my passions in my career every day! I just want to keep on keeping on as I play to win!

As we progress, you will deepen your personal awareness through various forms of introspection. Once all the exercises are complete, we will consolidate them into a framework for building your life on fire.

Remember to log in online and update your Quest!

Exercise: FBGM Aptitude and Personality Type

In business and in life, we should apply a similar common sense. The extroverts might like to "play in traffic" by networking to meet new prospective clients, while the introverts might build a more magnetic approach to business acquisition through online resources.

Do you know your personality type?

Knowing your personality type is fun, but it can also be especially useful. Following *The Q4 Quest* book for this next exercise, Finder / Binder / Grinder / Minder, or FBGM, turns this information into practical application. Beginning with your Myers-Briggs personality type and concluding with your personalized FBGM Quest implementation, learn how to do more of what you do well and less of what you do not enjoy.

Check up from the neck up: Before we begin this exercise, consider the following question. On a scale of one to ten, with one being "not at all" and ten being "perfectly", how well do you know your personality style and where it thrives?

[1 - 2 - 3 - 4 - 5 - 6 - 7 - 8 - 9 - 10]

Using the links below, start by taking the online Myers-Briggs assessment. Remember, there are no right or wrong answers, and one type is not better than another. After that, you can apply *The Q4 Quest* proprietary FBGM overlay to further develop your personality framework.

Start here:

1. Go to https://www.16personalities.com/free-personality-test and take your free personality test.
   - Remember, be honest—there are no wrong answers
2. Record your answer here: _____
   - Remember that for our purposes, we are focused specifically on your *sales* team aptitude. For a holistic review of your personality, see https://www.16personalities.com/personality-types
   - Clearly, some types will appear made for certain roles. There are also certainly exceptions to every rule. If you are drawn to a position that seems to be outside of your traditional type, that merely means you should be conscious of how your personal characteristics might influence you in that role.
3. Now, find yourself on the following chart and circle or highlight your sales aptitude summary below.

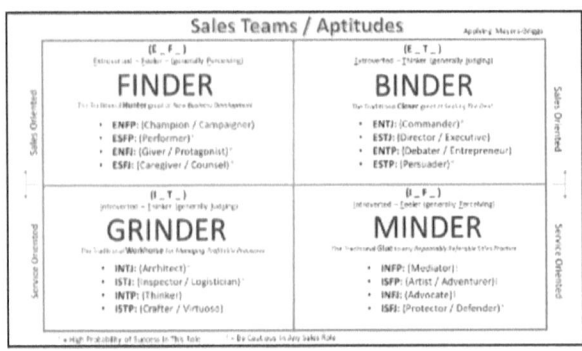

The Q4 Quest for Financial Advisors

Note: Finders and Binders generally fall on the direct sales side of a sales team coin while Grinders and Minders typically fall on the service side of a sales team.

Review the following descriptions and circle your type:

1. **Finder – A traditional sales Hunter is great at developing new business. They can also close and service, but get bogged down in the details and should consider adding a service component to the business to begin with, followed by a Binder as the growth warrants.**
    a. **ENFP – (Champions)** are natural leaders and often skilled salespeople as well because they are outgoing, likable, and charismatic. They believe in doing what is right and have strong inner morals, which are very personal to them. If this person does not believe in the product or process, they will get frustrated quickly and will struggle in the position, feeling drained by the situation. They can be the best in their field but need a supportive team and a mission-driven atmosphere.
    b. **ESFP* – (Performers)** are outgoing and fun people to be around, which makes them excellent salespeople. They know how to make the experience fun for others, and their disposition makes others excited about a product. They often take time to ask questions and will use those details to build the relationship. They often work well on a team, especially with great leaders and support staff.
    c. **ENFJ* – (Givers)** are often excellent salespeople because they are personable and know how to communicate with people in a way that creates a comfortable environment. They love helping others but may lose interest in a position at times in search of greater meaning. They can also thrive in a sales role if it emphasizes relationships and a more altruistic mission.
    d. **ESFJ*– (Caregivers)** are often excellent salespeople. They are friendly, compassionate, and great at reading people and their buying signs. They connect with someone almost effortlessly and use this ability to convince others the product they have

is perfect for them. These people can seem domineering on a team and reckless, but with support and room to run, they can enjoy the competitive nature and will not be afraid to lead.

2. **Binder – A traditional sales closer great at sealing the deal. They can also hunt and service but can get burned out or overwhelmed with the day-to-day and should consider adding a service component to the business to begin with, followed by one or more finders as the growth warrants.**
    a. **ENTJ* – (Commanders)** are typically skilled at presenting themselves in a way that is easily understood. Their skills make them excellent at closing deals and navigating business politics, and they will quickly climb "the ladder." to being among the best of the best. These types can seem domineering to those that feel threatened by their drive for excellence, but as part of a team or sole practitioner they will do as much work and research as possible to be well versed in whatever they are selling.
    b. **ESTJ – (Directors)** may be decent salespeople because they are competitive, charismatic, and sociable. They will also do their best to learn how to sell a specific product to people. These types like to learn and work as part of a team. Their drive for knowledge and often limited ability to feel for the client may make them better closers than traditional hunters. Their thirst for recognition makes them very capable of being among the best if they desire.
    c. **ENTP – (Debaters)** can be good salespeople because they are charismatic and intelligent. They can learn what they need to beat the competition and have the skills to connect well with others. These types may prefer to be closer to be a hunter because they are usually easily distracted and struggle with maintaining the daily discipline for constancy. As part of a team, they can be just the right touch to close deals once they have been cultivated.
    d. **ESTP* - (Persuaders)** are often some of the best salespeople in their field because they are charming and outgoing people. They are not afraid to become a little pushy to make a sale and

can maintain a connection while doing so. This type, maybe more than any other, thrives in awkward situations and going head-to-head with cut-throat situations where their charisma and competitive nature often wins the day.

3. **Grinder – A traditional workhorse on the service side of a sales team. Great at developing, maintaining, and improving systems and processes and ideal for an established business or part of a disciplined two-sided team. They can also close sales if necessary but will avoid hunting if possible through creative strategies to accomplish sales such as marketing, cross-selling, and retention. They should partner with a Finder or Binder as soon as possible and look to add a minder as growth warrants.**

    a. **INTJ* – (Architects)** can handle a sales position, but generally work best as part of a team because they will likely research all the requirements necessary to help a client. These introverts are usually happier in a more private work setting, but can overcome this to get things done for a mission. Ideally these people design processes for uncovering opportunities within existing relationships and can drive revenue in a background setting very effectively.

    b. **ISTJ* – (Inspectors)** are very capable people who will find a way to be the best at what they do. However, they may not find themselves naturally interested in sales. These introverts also dislike feeling forced to interact and sell to people, since they prefer to work in a more private setting. As part of a team working behind the scenes, they will enjoy finding ways to make the team better, and often bring fresh insight to a situation overlooked by more traditional pacesetters.

    c. **INTP – (Thinkers)** are rarely seen as salespeople and often dislike having to interface with people daily. These types generally despise the thought of traditional sales, which also makes them skilled at finding creative ways to sell to people that bring the people to them and their team.

    d. **ISTP – (Crafters)** are charming people who know how to sell to others but do not stay excited about being out in front. These types especially dislike handling award situations or

annoying people. Traditional sales can become exhausting for them because they prefer to be on their own most of the time. However, if allowed to be creative they can develop new strategies for growing a business.
4. **Minder – The glue to any relationship-driven practice falling on the service side of a sales team. They are great at duplicating best clients through acts of sincere appreciation. Minders are necessary for growing any established business, but also a great part of a disciplined two-sided team. They can also close sales if necessary and are eager to try. They should partner with a Finder or Binder as soon as possible and look to add a grinder as growth warrants.**
    a. **INFP – (Mediators)** are not salespeople and simply despise the job itself. These types do not enjoy having to push someone to purchase a product, and view sales as manipulative and possibly against their morals. They always want to do what is right and generally cannot see the necessity of a sale. If they are required to sell, they will have a hard time doing so and may even resist. As part of a sales team, they may excel at serving existing clients with education if they can connect clients to those who will persuade them to act.
    b. **ISFP – (Artists)** are not salespeople and any attempt to make them will exhaust this person. If this type is made to make a sale, they will often resist, calling sales immoral and ultimately tiring. These types also need plenty of time to themselves to recharge and cannot generally maintain the activity necessary for consistent sales. As part of the client service or appreciation component of a team, they can apply their compassion and creativity to make clients feel warm about the organization, which may lead to referrals and new sales.
    c. **INFJ – (Advocates)** are not often interested in sales and might find that role sketchy. These types need their work to feel warm to be fulfilling. Like other introverts, these types find sales draining and even emotionally damaging. They do not see sales as making a difference in the world and cannot appreciate the role it plays in business. If this type must sell,

they are intelligent and capable of doing so and have a knack for reading people which will help them to succeed. However, these advocates are best behind a team advocating for the client's best interests and supporting the team with their intuition.

d. **ISFJ* – (Protectors)** are friendly and have a kind demeanor, making them good at working with people. These introverts can certainly sell a product, but they can become a bit drained by constant social interaction. These types are not particularly good at the "art" of sales and avoid awkward or pushy situations, often believing them to be underhanded maneuvers by their colleagues used to beat them. These types often blend kindness and healthy skepticism, which makes this person an ideal part of a team's client service model. Always cautious that they could be doing more, they lead with love can drive the relationship process if they have the right supporting personalities around them.

Record your FBGM aptitude here.

```
Myers Briggs: _____
B / B / G / M : _____
```

(Bonus) Additional introspection

- What personality types do you have around you that could be leveraged to catapult your practice?
- What types do you still need to find, add, or develop to your process to maximize your success?
- What actions might you take to start strengthening your team?

Check up from the neck up: After completing this exercise, consider the following question. On a scale of one to ten, with one being "not at all" and ten being "perfectly", how well do you feel you are efficiently maximizing your personality strengths while incubating your more challenging areas?

[1 - 2 - 3 - 4 - 5 - 6 - 7 - 8 - 9 - 10]

The foundation for the Q4 Quest begins with understanding, and given the exercise, how well do you feel you can lay some bricks? (check one)

- ☐ **Low** – I can see many areas where I am not best utilizing my strengths. I am tired of struggling with things I do not enjoy when I know there are areas I can excel in.
- ☐ **Medium** – I understand the personalities, and could do a better job of playing to win. I am eager to change my systems and processes so I can do more of what I was made to do and do well.
- ☐ **High** – I am aware of how these personalities work and have already begun building my team around this information. I am excited to expand on what I am learning.

As we progress, you will deepen your personal awareness through various forms of introspection. Once all the exercises are complete, we will consolidate them into a framework for building a life you are on fire for.

Remember to log in online and update your Quest.

Exercise: Personal Past - Part A

The following exercise will help you pull a defining event or theme out of your past that has shaped how you tell your story today. The difference between a basic biography and a magnetic marketing statement is found in

The Q4 Quest for Financial Advisors

your ability to tell your story well. Our private clients often spend hours, weeks, even months perfecting this process, but you can begin your story right here.

Check up from the neck up: Before we begin this exercise, consider the following question. On a scale of one to ten, with one being "not at all" and ten being "perfect", how well does your story capture your contestability? (circle one)

[1 - 2 - 3 - 4 - 5 - 6 - 7 - 8 - 9 - 10]

Consider the following questions and craft your own story. Be human, be approachable, maybe even vulnerable. People connect with people, not canned text.

- What trial or event have you triumphed that fuels your passion or practice today?
- Can you define your event in just a few words?
- Now, being more specific, how does this event still shape who you are today?
- What audience might be most attracted to your story and insight?
- How do you capture that in your business, marketing, and other relationships?

Write your "Past" here.

Check up from the neck up: After completing this exercise, consider the following question. On a scale of one to ten, with one being "not at all" and ten being "perfect", how magnetic is your story? (circle one)

[1 - 2 - 3 - 4 - 5 - 6 - 7 - 8 - 9 - 10]

Your personal past is a powerful weapon in your journey of life. How well are you telling a story that captures the hearts and minds of your ideal client? (check one)

- ☐ **Low** – I have put little effort into becoming relatable, let alone magnetic. I need to work in this area and am ready to dive in.
- ☐ **Medium** – I have a bio and am decent at connecting with new people, but I could use work refining that story to be more magnetic.
- ☐ **High** – I excel in this area and lead with my heart on my sleeve. I am glad to see that this is a good characteristic, and I am excited to build on it.

Again, as we progress, you will deepen your personal awareness through various forms of introspection. Once all the exercises are complete, we will consolidate them into a framework for building a life you are on fire for.

Remember to log in online and update your Quest!

Exercise: Present Story – Part B (Be Magnetic)

Now it's time to get magnetic.

Using all that we have learned so far, write your own magnetic marketing biography.

- Perhaps you may just need to rework existing generic information you have with more provoking and personal information. Others may want to start fresh with all this added introspection.
- Remember to make it personal because people are more likely to seek out relationships with people they can relate to.

Check up from the neck up: Before we begin this exercise, consider the following question. On a scale of one to ten, with one being "not at all" and ten being "perfect", how magnetic is your story in showing how unique your process is to business and bringing the customers it deserves? (circle one)

[1 - 2 - 3 - 4 - 5 - 6 - 7 - 8 - 9 - 10]

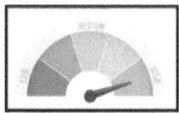

On one to two pages, write your concise but thorough biography, remembering to include highlights from the following questions:

- Who matters most to you?
    - (Consider including multiple tiers from your six-tiers of relational influence).
- What matters most to you?
    - (Consider highlighting your personal vision and mission as well as any unique professional priorities)
- Your relevant passions and gifts.
    - (Consider anything that might make you relatable to your ideal audiences).
- Your past.
    - (Any events that make you approachable by your ideal audiences).

For example:

(Name) (relationships (more detailed the better)). (Personal vision and mission statement) (Any achievements related to the life you're trying to build). (State your passion). (Anything that drives you into your ideal audiences). (Any events that make you approachable).

Write your "Bio" here.

Check up from the neck up: After completing this exercise, consider the following question. On a scale of one to ten, with one being "not at all" and ten being "perfect", how well does your biography magnetically reflect your story in a way that captures and captivates your target markets? (circle one)

[1 - 2 - 3 - 4 - 5 - 6 - 7 - 8 - 9 - 10]

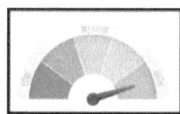

How do you feel about your bio's ability to differentiate you from your would-be peers? (check one)

☐ **Low** – My bio sounds like everyone else's. I even used a cliché canned text to get started, but I am ready to change to magnetic marketing.

- ☐ **Medium** – I have a bio that tells my story well, but I have done little to capitalize on it within my marketing efforts. I am open to exploring new ways to develop this process.
- ☐ **High** – I have put a lot of thought and time into my bio and am ready to incorporate it better into my practice and my process.

Remember, as we progress, you will deepen your personal awareness through various forms of introspection. Once all the exercises are complete, we will consolidate them into a framework for building a life that you are on fire for.

Remember to log in online and update your Quest!

Exercise: Resources – Time

There is only so much time in a day. If you want to earn more, you can either work harder or work smarter.

Check up from the neck up: Before we begin this exercise, consider the following question. On a scale of one to ten, with one being "not at all" and ten being "perfect", how well do you know what your time is worth per hour professionally? (circle one)

[1 - 2 - 3 - 4 - 5 - 6 - 7 - 8 - 9 - 10]

If you are like most business owners and financial advisors, you are already working hard and have little bandwidth left to work harder, so the choice is made for you. You need to work smarter. To do that, begin by understanding your EPH or earning per hour.

There are many ways to calculate this number, and the more complex your business structure and employees, the more complex your calculations may need to be, but the basic math works like this:

Divide the amount of income you project earning this year by 2,000 (50 weeks x 40 hours per week doing client engagement).

_____$150,000____ / 2,000 = ____$75_____ per hour.

As we discussed in the Q4 Quest, you must also account for the number of service hours a typical client takes. Of course, the answer depends on your specialty, demographic, and service model, but as a rule-of-thumb, the average A client takes twelve to eighteen hours a year to service, including travel, prep, review, and service calls. (Precisely why a solo practitioner or small practice does not have room to properly serve more than about a hundred clients at a time and still have time to manage the other business activities essential to managing a practice).

Early in your career, it may have been a race to get your first clients, but as you grow, that sprint becomes a marathon, and the tools that made you a success early on are not the same tools that you will need to refine to sustain new success.

Exercise: Resources – Time

Take a moment now to find your own target EPH (earnings per hour).

- Divide the amount of income you project earning this year by the number of hours you anticipate working. (2,000 represents fifty weeks at forty hours per week)

Earnings: _____ / 2,000 = _____ per hour.

Now, how many hours does a typical client take? Perhaps you have multiple service models? Find an average if necessary but focus on A-clients. (Average 'A' client takes 12-15 hours a year to serve.) Or, using the previous example. What is your minimum target revenue per client (not adjusting for operational expenses)?

$$75 \times 15 = \underline{\hspace{2in}}.$$

- **How many clients can you serve in 2000 hours leaving time for operations?** _____
- **How many clients do you have?** _____
- **How many clients pay you what you are worth?** _____
- **Using the previous example, how many clients do you have that earn you less than your target EPH, and are effectively costing you money to maintain?**

$$\underline{\hspace{0.5in} 12 \times ?\hspace{3in}}$$

Additional considerations:

- **How many hours does a typical client take?** Perhaps you have multiple service models? Find an average if necessary, but focus on A-clients.
- **How many clients can you serve?** _____
- **And how many clients do you already have?** _____

In our private coaching, we review this area, our service models, and the "escalator" growth models extensively. However, time management begins here by knowing AND sticking to your desired EPH.

Check up from the neck up: After completing this exercise, consider the following question. On a scale of one to ten, with one being "not at all" and ten being "perfect", how well are you managing your practice according to your EPH? (circle one)

[1 - 2 - 3 - 4 - 5 - 6 - 7 - 8 - 9 - 10]

How well do you manage your practice with your EPH? (check one)

- ☐ **Low** – I am still taking anyone who says yes, but I know I need to do better. I am ready to get serious about growth.
- ☐ **Medium** – I have started implementing this strategy, but I am not able to let anyone go for fear of my bottom line, or because I am emotionally attached to them. I am open to exploring this more, but will need help to navigate these hang-ups.
- ☐ **High** – I have a disciplined service model, I know what I am worth per hour professionally, and I generally adhere to it. I just need help to apply this to growth acceleration, such as the "escalator model" discussed in some private coaching I have heard about.

Again, as we progress, you will be deepening your personal awareness through various forms of introspection. Once all the exercises are complete, we will consolidate them into a framework for building your life on fire.

Remember to log in online and update your Quest!

Exercise: Resources – Money

As we learned from our Quest, time and money are two sides of the same coin, and one impacts the other. To help you make sound decisions with your business, it is imperative, much like financial planning, to know where you are, where you are going, and how you are getting there. For new businesses, this section can be more challenging, however, for practices with a few years under their belts, these are perfect exercises to manage for growth rather than just running full speed and hoping for the best!

Check up from the neck up: Before we begin this exercise, consider the following question. On a scale of one to ten, with one being "not at all" and ten being "perfect", how well can you accurately forecast your growth? (circle one)

[1 - 2 - 3 - 4 - 5 - 6 - 7 - 8 - 9 - 10]

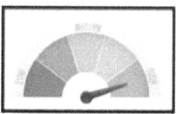

Exercise: Resources – Money

Take a moment now to find your growth rate, first by assets and then by income.

This section is actually a three-part exercise. A) Using the following chart as a guide, begin with a simple calculation of your existing assets, and projected growth rates.

A) AUM Forecasting

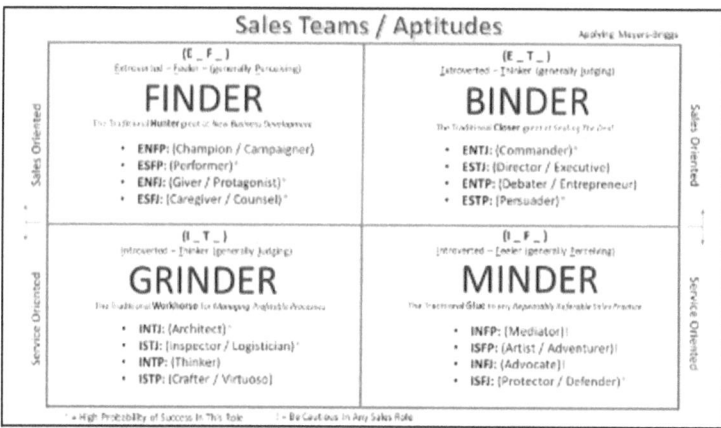

With this information, you can start to project next year's growth based on your situation.

Now B) by determining your run rate, that is the amount of revenue you earn off each dollar invested with you (as an average), you can also start to project your cash flow.

B) Run rate and this year's forecasted revenue.

Net New Asset Number. (New assets less withdraws, transfers, markets, and attrition)	Example	You
Assets Under Management (AUM) at the beginning of LAST year:	$22,000,000	
AUM at the end of the Year:	$31,000,000	
Growth Rate in terms of a percentage % (Increase ÷ Original Number × 100):	41%	
(AUM) beginning of THIS year (Same as end of last year):	$31,000,000	
Growth Rate assuming previous years %:	$43,681,818	
Adjust for AUM lost each year due to transfers, deaths, RMD's, and other anticipated withdraws:	-$3,000,000	
AUM Trend	$40,681,818	
Adjust for anticipated market movement in your forecasting (Add or subtract %):	5%	
Forecasted AUM at Year End:	$42,715,909	
Increase	38%	

In our private coaching, we spend more time on strategies for increasing run rates while improving your client's realized value.

To start, update your profile now, and for further development visit the workbook section of this Quest and update your profile online.

C) Reinvestment (rules-of-thumb) fifty/thirty/twenty

Now we come to the third and final part of this section: reinvestment rules-of-thumb. Building a budget is outside the scope of this book, and may be unnecessary. However, what is necessary is remembering the business is both a lifestyle and an investment and should, at a minimum, follow the rule of fifty/thirty/twenty rule.

This means fifty percent should be considered for needs, including base salaries and business expenses. Thirty percent should be considered for business wants, including marketing (including seminars and client events), equipment, and improving infrastructure, with twenty percent being put into savings, including operating funds, insurance, and succession.

	Run Rate (Target .80 - 1.00)	Example	You
	Last Year Total Commission as Gross Dealer Concession (GDC):	$140,000	
	AUM at the end of the Year:	$31,000,000	
	Run Rate (GDC / AUM)	0.45%	
	Forecasted AUM (From Above)	$42,715,909	
	GDC based on current Run Rate	$192,911	
	Payout (Grid rate)	70%	
	Net Earning before Expenses	$135,037	

- Any revenue that exceeds early projections can be taken as a bonus above the base salary or reinvested into the business growth or both.

We often find that many young practices extract too much money to maintain salaries, and then struggle to reinvest in proper marketing, staff, and infrastructure. These practices often do well until they do not, and once they start to sink, there are not enough oars to stay afloat, and they go under or change careers.

In our private coaching, we address this in detail. For our disciplined clients serious about treating their career as a business and not a sales marathon, we also spend more time on monitoring marketing activities for maximizing return on investment (ROI) and minimizing costs of acquisition (COA).

For now, build a strong foundation and update your profile. For further development, visit the workbook section of this Quest and update your profile online.

Check up from the neck up: After completing this exercise, consider the following question. On a scale of one to ten, with one being "not at all" and ten being "perfect", how well do you manage your practices cash flow? (circle one)

[1 - 2 - 3 - 4 - 5 - 6 - 7 - 8 - 9 - 10]

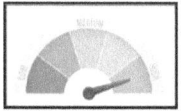

Describe your practice's fiscal management prowess here. (check one)

- ☐ **Low** – Up until now, I have just kept my head down and focused on daily sales activity. I am now ready to work "on" my business as much as "in" my business.
- ☐ **Medium** – I look at this information when I do business planning, but I could do a better job of allowing the data to drive my priorities and subsequent success.

☐ **High** – I am on top of these numbers regularly and excited to learn more about how to use this information to drive future success.

Like before, as we progress, you will deepen your personal awareness through various forms of introspection. Once all the exercises are complete, we will consolidate them into a framework for building a life you are on fire for.

Remember to log in online and update your Quest!

Exercise: Resources – Relationships

When we stop thinking of everything as a numbers game and start seeing everyone as a true relationship and opportunity to serve, energy starts to flow, and great things happen. In short, the Q4 Quest comes from a proper understanding that we are all in one business . . . the relationship business. Specifically, the Q4 Quest looks at our relationships through three lenses: personal, professional, and positional.

- **Personal relationships** are those closest to you, those in your inner circle, like family, friends, and any of your closest business partners. You may recall the relationship mapping exercises earlier in your quest. We started there for a reason because relationships are your number one resource. If I took all your money away, but you had relationships, you would be okay in the end. If, however, I isolate you from everyone forever, even with all the money in the world you would still be in prison.
- **Professional Relationships** are those outside your key employees. These may be referral partners from a networking group or accountants who know and utilize your skills with their best clients or other industry-related influencers. These relationships are often discovered and deepened through your best clients, and for that reason you should focus initially on developing your best existing relationships.

- **Positional Relationships** are the key and the difference between growing by twenty percent through grunt work or growing by as much as 80 percent or more and having a blast the whole time. These relationships are your top clients and best cheerleaders. They fully utilize and appreciate your value and introduce you to others such as their CPAs, lawyers, peers, family, and friends. Like the example of the cross-disciplinary lunch and learn – these relationships have other advisors, complicated situations, and understand the value of paying for good advice.

Think about it like this. When the phone rings, there are those who you can't wait to talk to, and then there are those who you roll your eyes at. These clients are the former, and your goal is to lead the team of their inner circle to a new value while earning new sources of revenue and ultimately new trusted referrals, which we prefer to call "introductions."

So, before you can jump out there and start duplicating your best clients (think about how cool that is in itself!), you need to complete your prep work.

Check up from the neck up: Before we begin this exercise, consider the following question. On a scale of one to ten, with one being "not at all" and ten being "perfect", how well do you feel you know all the levels of your existing relationships? (circle one)

[1 - 2 - 3 - 4 - 5 - 6 - 7 - 8 - 9 - 10]

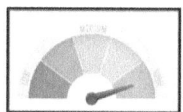

Exercise: Relationships

Using the following chart as a guide, begin to aggregate your households by consolidating all individual accounts relating to a particular family and business. For example, an IRA, college savings account, insurance policy should all be 'household' Invest the time necessary to do this for all relationships.

(Note that a household may represent multiple accounts (husband, wife, business retirement, and a college fund, for example).

You will be able to determine which clients are ideal for duplicating, and how they can help you to do so.

Household	Total Accounts	Total Gross Revenue (Rolling 12)	Transactional / First Year Only Fees	Retired / Employed	Business Owner	Recurring Revenue / Investments	Recurring Revenue / Insurance	Recurring Revenue / Planning	Projected (Recurring Rev combined)	Retirement Income Planning	Estate Planning / Tax	Business Succession and Insurance	Health Insurance and Benefits Review	Personal Life and Long-Term Care	Education & Generational Planning	Charitable Planning	Goals Planning	Special Needs Planning	Relationship (Hot/Warm/Cold/None/Self) - Tax	Relationship (Hot/Warm/Cold/None/Self) - Legal	Relationship (Hot/Warm/Cold/None/Self) - Insurance	Relationship (Hot/Warm/Cold/None/Self) - Investment	Relationship (Hot/Warm/Cold/None/Self) - Planning	Relationship (Hot/Warm/Cold/None/Self) - Benefits	Relationship (Hot/Warm/Cold/None/Self) - Banking
1. Mr. and Mrs. Fancy Pants	4	$23,000	$6,300	Emp.	Yes	$10,000	$4,200	$2,500	$16,700	Done	Need	Need	Need	Need	Need	Done		NA	Warm	None	self	self	self	self	self
2.																									
3.																									
4.																									
5.																									

– *Continue until all relationships are accounted for.*

Considerations:

- **How many households do you have?**
    - o Using the recurring revenue totals, how many households are paying you what you need to make according to your target EPH exercise?
    - o How many are you allowing to hold you back?
- **How many opportunities do you have to increase your value to your top clients?**
    - o How many opportunities do you have with existing clients below your target EPH that can be revisited?
    - o How many of your clients have generational, estate, or special needs planning that you have not yet done that could lead to new relationships?
    - o How many business owner clients do you have that could lead to employee benefits and retirement relationships?

- **How many of your top relationships have other professionals that you could be deepening by driving holistic team meetings?**
    - o How many of your smaller transactional clients could benefit from cross-discipline planning and may have the potential to cross over your target EPH?
    - o How many are not likely to ever reach your target EPH and need to be managed accordingly? (through automated service models, raising fees, or partnering)

In our private coaching, we address these strategies in more detail. However, just getting a handle on your situation can highlight dozens of opportunities for new services and revenue, and just as many new relationships for duplicating your best clients.

Start now and build a strong foundation through data and organization.

Check up from the neck up: After completing this exercise, consider the following question. On a scale of one to ten, with one being "not at all" and ten being "perfect", how well do you manage your relationships to grow your practice? (circle one)

[1 - 2 - 3 - 4 - 5 - 6 - 7 - 8 - 9 - 10]

Describe your practice's fiscal management prowess here. (check one)

- ☐ **Low** – I have not had time to slow down and deepen relationships with my existing clients. I know I need to do this, and I am eager to get started!
- ☐ **Medium** – I know my clients well, but I need help penetrating their friends, family, and circles of influence. When do we start?
- ☐ **High** – I know my clients, their kids, their parents, their friends, and their key advisors. I love this stuff and just need to learn strategies for getting better personal introductions.

Just like before, as we progress, you will deepen your personal awareness through various forms of introspection. Now we can consolidate what we have and strengthen our framework for our practice and our life.

Remember to log in online and update your Quest!

Q3 – Conclusion

The exercises above give you the bricks to lay your pathway to actualizing your Q4 Quest. You leave this chapter ahead of most of your peers and with more clarity than ever before. We conclude with the tools help you now run towards your goals.

Prioritization

In the section, Situation, we worked through multiple areas. Looking back at each of the exercises in that section, consolidate your rankings below.

"Quest-o-meter"

	Low	Medium	High
Passion Assessment			
FBGM Aptitude and personality test			
Past			
Present Story			
Resources: time			
Resources: money			
Resources: relationships			

Check up from the neck up: On a scale of one to ten, with one being "needs work" and ten being "near perfect", before you began this Quest how complete and methodical was your "situation?"

[1 - 2 - 3 - 4 - 5 - 6 - 7 - 8 - 9 - 10]

Now, using that same scale, how much clearer are your practice processes and potential?

[1 - 2 - 3 - 4 - 5 - 6 - 7 - 8 - 9 - 10]

Now, what would it take to move your business even a fraction of a number closer to perfect? (say from a six to a 6.5?)

So, when do we start?

Horizon (Or Look Back Test) Test

Finally, we jump onto the journey and start to live a truly Q4 life. Using the Horizon test below, let us make sure we haven't missed the forest for the trees by answering a few engagement questions.

- Five years from now, or even one year from now, if we were to reflect on your life, comparing it to where it is today, what things would you have had to change that would demonstrate the benefit of our journey together?
- Now, on a scale of one to ten (ten being the greatest), rate the following:
    - ➢ _____ Before we started working on this, how satisfied were you with your path's potential?
    - ➢ _____ After you have completed this work, how satisfied are you?
    - ➢ _____ What's the first thing that you will do, or notice from your initial progress?
    - ➢ _____ What one thing can you do not to bump your satisfaction for even a fraction of a percent today?

Remember to be realistic. This is a marathon, not a sprint. In fact, when we are living, the authentic journey is the destination. There is no such thing as 110 percent. In fact, even at one hundred percent we will inevitably burn out or be forced to give everything only a fraction of our focus and energy, or both.

Exercise: Quick Litmus Test/Reverse Check-Up

Like checking answers in a math class, you can easily check your decision and your journey with a quick life check-up by simply looking back on your journey in reverse.

Ask yourself, do the decisions you are making today:

- Align with your priorities (Expectations)
- Utilize your gifts and resources (Situation)
- Passionately enhance your personal mission and vision for the world (Reservations)
- and provide and protect the people who matter most to you (Motivations)?

"Do the decisions you are making today align with your priorities in a way that utilizes your gifts and resources, while passionately enhancing your mission and vision for the world and providing and protecting the people you say matter most?"

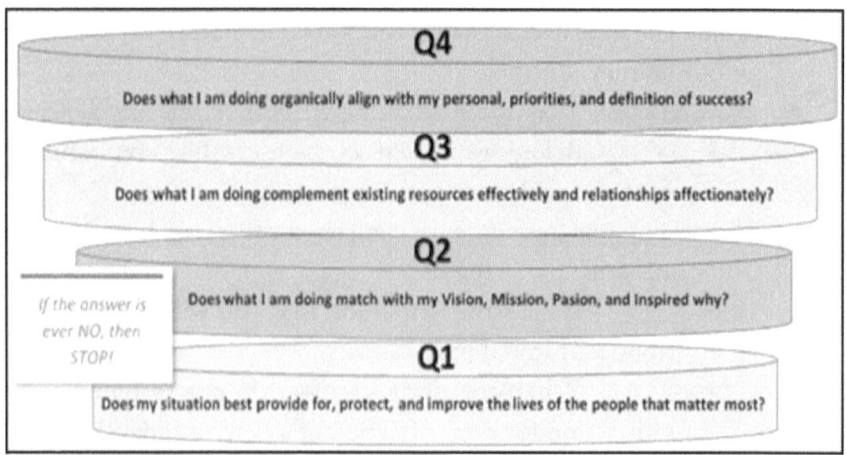

So, when do we start?

Q4

EXPECTATION

The fourth and final step to the Q4 Quest, is about having clearly defined expectations. After all, if you do not know where you're going, how will you know when you get there? Likewise, if you do not have a map, how will you know if you get off track? This step now pulls everything together and prepares you to play to win on your terms—no one else's.

Expectations

Look back at all the work you have put into the who, how, and what of your journey. It would be a shame to not use the information you have gained by not putting it into action. After all, this is the Q4 Quest. It is about the journey. Life is to be lived, not just observed. This last section's final exercises ultimately give your data a direction to go. So let us round third and start heading home.

Exercise: The Three Eulogies

Check up from the neck up: Before we begin this exercise, consider the following question. On a scale of one to ten, with one being "not at all" and ten beings "perfectly", how well do you feel your life today represents a legacy you would be proud to be remembered for? (circle one)

[1 - 2 - 3 - 4 - 5 - 6 - 7 - 8 - 9 - 10]

Exercise: The Three Eulogies

Using the Q4 Quest's story of the three eulogies as a springboard, look at the following exercise. You are at your own funeral or wake and listening in as three visitors represent your past, present, and future. All speak about your impact on them and the world. What might they say about it? Using the following questions as a guide, attempt to capture in writing what each of these eulogies might say about you.

(1) Past – Who is that one person (you can only pick one) who helped to make you who you are today?
- What kind of person would they say you were? Why did they like you?
- What impact on others or the world would they say your presence made?
- How would they highlight your journey together?
- Be boldly honest here. Why did they work with you? (What did they see in you that you have not seen in yourself?)
- At your memorial, what do you hope they would say about you that captures what made them most proud of you as a person?
- With honest introspection, and based on how you live today, what are those inconsistencies with how they see you and how you truly are?

(2) Present – Name the person (a peer, close friend, or mentor) who pours energy into you and challenges you to be the best version of yourself?
- What kind of person would they say you are?
- What impact on others or the world would they say your presence makes?
- How would they highlight your journey together?
- Be boldly honest here. Why do they enjoy working with you? (What positive attributes of your character do you think they see in you that you do not yet believe about yourself?)
- At your memorial, what do you hope they would say about you that captures what made them most proud of you as a person?
- With honest introspection, based on how you live today, what are those inconsistencies with how they will come to see you and how you truly are today?

(3) Future – From someone you know but could know better, or even one you have yet to meet (or at least develop a meaningful relationship with), who is a person you believe could challenge you to become a person you would like to work closely with? Imagining how they might pour into your life consider the following questions.
- What kind of person would you hope they say you are?
- What impact on others or the world would they say your presence made?
- How would they highlight your journey together?
- Be boldly honest here. Why would they want to work with you? What aspects of your character do you need to work on that might entice them to work with you?
- At your memorial, what do you hope they would say about you that captures what made them most proud of you as a person?

- With honest introspection, based on how you live today, what are those inconsistencies with who you hope they will see and how you live today?
- What has this exercise revealed to you about where you came from, where you are, and where you might go as a person?
- What inconsistencies might you see in how they see you, and how you see yourself living today?
- What changes might this exercise encourage?

In our private coaching, we address these strategies in more detail. The time put into self exploration pays dividends in growth, magnetic marketing, relationship building, and managing reservations.

Check up from the neck up: After completing this exercise, consider the following question. On a scale of one to ten, with one being "not at all" and ten being "perfect", how close does your current *life* reflect all you hope to be remembered for? (circle one)

[1 - 2 - 3 - 4 - 5 - 6 - 7 - 8 - 9 - 10]

Now, how close does your current *work* reflect what you hope to be remembered for? (circle one)

- ☐ **Low** – I have a long way to go to reach a legacy I might be proud of. I never really thought I could live a legacy filled life already. I am interested in learning how to better "live the dream!"

- ☐ **Medium** – I am starting to live the dream, but I have a long way to go. Let us dive deeper!
- ☐ **High** – I am living the dream and loving the ride. I would love to explore ways to expand my significance or protect my sustainability against death, disability, or other contingencies.

Now that all the exercises are completed, we are consolidating them to help us frame and maintain motivation while providing daily clarity and accountability. This section sets our perspective.

Exercise: Self, Service, Or Stuff

How do you define success? This might be thought of as your professional "Love Language."

- Are you driven by self-actualization and progress? (Self)
- Or perhaps you are most passionate about helping others? (Service)
- Or maybe you chase a certain lifestyle? (Stuff)

Exercise: Self, Service, Or Stuff

The reality is you probably are driven by elements of all three, but probably not in equal proportion.

Check up from the neck up: Before we begin this exercise, consider the following question. On a scale of one to ten, with one being "not at all" and ten being "perfectly", how well do you understand your primary reinforcers (Self, Service, Stuff)? (circle one)

[1 - 2 - 3 - 4 - 5 - 6 - 7 - 8 - 9 - 10]

In the spirit of all that we have done so far, take another minute and put a quantifiable measure of what constitutes success in your own life. Now, using the chart below, consider the three areas of self-stuff-service and follow the instructions outlined.

1) Rank them in order of personal preference with one being the most important, and the being the third in importance. Remember, this is your journey and not the Joneses. If all you want is a fast car today, then say so. Inversely, if you just want to help the homeless regardless of your personal financial situation, then say that. The only wrong answer is a lie.
2) Demonstrate how you might categorize these three priorities by using chips; spreading them out across each of the three boxes below. You can spread them evenly or put them all in one box. Just be honest.
3) Lastly, make bullet points about any specific priorities you have in the appropriate box such as a specific bucket list trip, or ideal home, or the new Cruiser.

	Self	**Stuff**	**Service**
Includes:	Influence / Accolades	Lifestyle	Impact / Legacy
Rank:	1 / 2 / 3	1 / 2 / 3	1 / 2 / 3
Chips: 1-9			
Specific Goals			

In our private coaching, we address these strategies in more detail. The time put into self-exploration pays dividends in growth, magnetic marketing, relationship building, and managing reservations.

Check up from the neck up: After completing this exercise, consider the following question. On a scale of one to ten, with one being "not at all" and ten being "perfectly", how well are you rewarding yourself appropriately through your primary reinforcers? (circle one)

[1 - 2 - 3 - 4 - 5 - 6 - 7 - 8 - 9 - 10]

Describe how well you think you utilize these reinforcers in your business. (Check one)

- ☐ **Low** – I have not tied my reinforcers to my business plan but would like to start now.
- ☐ **Medium** – I do a decent job of rewarding myself appropriately, but I could use work, making it more meaningful.
- ☐ **High** – I pay close attention to my personal reinforcers and run my business accordingly. I am ready to pass that structure on to my staff or partners.

Now all the exercises are completed, we are consolidating them to help us frame and maintain motivation while providing daily clarity and accountability. This section adds clarity.

Exercise: Priority Path

Prioritization

As we said during the Quest, every journey begins with a single step so let's move our feet! Left or right is your choice but pick one and move it!

It is time to look back up. Your mission and your vision should lead the way. This is what we call the north star. To get you moving in the right direction, or just moving at all, we ask you to think about starting your Q4 Quest today. What would be the first step?

Think about where your life is today and on a scale of one to ten, with one being perfect, where do you feel your life is today? Now, what would it take to move your life even a fraction of a number closer to perfect? Say from a six to a 6.5? Write that down. In fact, looking back at everything we have covered, you can consolidate all your action steps so we can build a priority pathway for your personal Q4 Quest.

To help you consider using TRAMS goals so that we end with an action step towards a dream rather than a dream to take action.

These are goals that are specific, measurable, and relevant to your personal journey and no one else's. Look back over everything we have discussed, especially your motivations and relationship mapping, begin to lay down your TRAMS goals.

Time-bound
Relevant
Attainable
Measurable
Specific

Revisiting each of your Q4 Quest exercises, list all of your TRAMS goals here

Check up from the neck up: Before we begin this exercise, consider the following question. On a scale of one to ten, with one being "not at all" and ten being "perfectly", how well do you understand how to create impactful and organized goals with the information you've gathered? (circle one)

[1 - 2 - 3 - 4 - 5 - 6 - 7 - 8 - 9 - 10]

The Q4 Quest for Financial Advisors

We now move to the final part of your Quest development—the Priority Pathway.

Using the pathway exercise below, you may now bring everything together into a visual workflow and personal journey.

Take time to revisit each exercise and look for inconsistencies in how you have been living and the life you know you were made for. Make a list of necessary actions prioritized from highest to lowest until all changes have been accounted for.

(It may be helpful for some to consider completing one path for your personal life and a separate one for your professional life).

Priority Pathway

Now you have collected all of your relevant goals, we move to the final part of your Quest development—the Priority Pathway. Using the pathway exercise below, you may now bring everything together into a visual workflow and personal journey. *(It may be helpful for some to consider completing one path for your personal life and a separate one for your professional life).*

Priority Pathway

Take time to revisit each exercise and look for inconsistencies in how you have been living and the life you know you were made for. Make a list of necessary actions prioritized from highest to lowest until all changes have been accounted for. In our private coaching, we address these strategies in more detail. But for further help, visit the workbook in the back or *The Q4 Quest* online.

Check up from the neck up: After completing this exercise, consider the following question. On a scale of one to ten, with one being "not at all" and ten being "perfectly", how well do you now understand your personal path's priorities? (circle one)

[1 - 2 - 3 - 4 - 5 - 6 - 7 - 8 - 9 - 10]

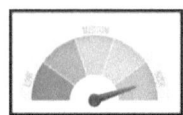

How ready are you to follow through with your own plan, and personal practices in business and in life? (check one)

- ☐ **Low** – I know now what I need to do, but I also know I rarely stay on point. I need more help to stay motivated and dedicated to my plan.
- ☐ **Medium** – I feel confident I can do this, but would appreciate all the help and motivation I can get.
- ☐ **High** – I love that I have a clear plan and am excited to have a daily driven discipline. As my mentor used to say, "flawless execution of a great plan all but ensures success!"

Now that all the exercises are complete, we can consolidate them to help us frame and maintain motivation while providing daily clarity and accountability. This section gives your quest direction!

Q4 – Conclusion

These last exercises have helped you to define your path while making your personal expectations clear. While society may have contributed to your current shortfalls, you have no excuse and no one to blame. The path is clear. Through the Q4 Quest you can now take the next step towards the life you know you were made for.

Prioritization

Looking back at each of the exercises in this section about "expectations," conclude by consolidating your priority rankings below.

"Quest-o-meter"

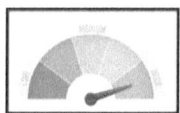

	Low	Medium	High
Three Eulogies			
Self, Service, Stuff			
Priority Pathway			

Check up from the neck up: On a scale of one to ten, with one being "needs work" and ten being "near perfect", before you began this Quest, how aware were you of your own expectations regarding rewards and accountability?"

[1 - 2 - 3 - 4 - 5 - 6 - 7 - 8 - 9 - 10]

Now, using that same scale, how much clearer are you today of what you should be focused on in your business?

[1 - 2 - 3 - 4 - 5 - 6 - 7 - 8 - 9 - 10]

Now, what would it take to move your business even a fraction of a number closer to perfect? (Say from a six to a 6.5?)

So, when do we start?

Horizon (Or Look Back Test) Test

Finally, we jump onto the journey and start to live a truly Q4 life. Using the Horizon test below, let us make sure we haven't missed the forest for the trees by answering a few engagement questions.

- If we were to reflect on your life in the future and compare it to where it is today, what things would you have had to change that would demonstrate the benefit of our journey together?
- Now, on a scale of one to ten (ten being the greatest) rate the following:
    - _____ Before we started working on this, how satisfied were you with your path's potential?
    - _____ After you have completed this work, how satisfied are you?
    - _____ What's the first thing that you will do, or notice from your initial progress?
    - _____ What one thing can you do not to bump your satisfaction for even a fraction of a percent today?

Remember to be realistic. This is a marathon, not a sprint. In fact, when we are living, the authentic journey is the destination. There is no such thing as 110 percent. In fact, even at one hundred percent, we will inevitably burn out or be forced to give everything only a fraction of our focus and energy, or both.

Exercise: Quick Litmus Test/Reverse Check-Up

Like checking answers in a math class, you can easily check your decision and your journey with a quick life check-up by simply looking back on your journey in reverse.

Ask yourself, do the decisions you are making today:

- Align with your priorities (Expectations)
- Utilize your gifts and resources (Situation),
- Passionately enhance your personal mission and vision for the world (Reservations),
- and provide and protect for the people who matter most to you (Motivations)?

> *"Do the decisions you are making today align with your priorities in a way that utilizes your gifts and resources, while passionately enhancing your mission and vision for the world and providing and protecting the people you say matter most?"*

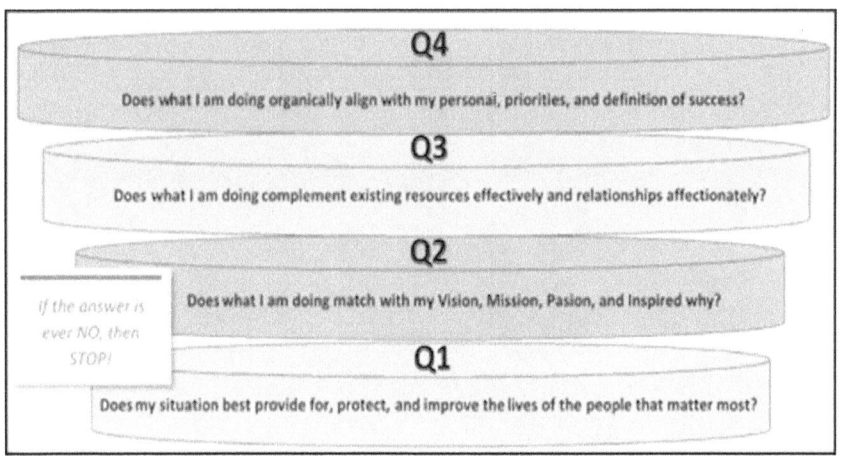

So, when do we start?

SPECIAL THANKS

The Q4 Quest is the culmination of decades of personal research, experience, and application built on timeless truths and great minds of the past. In addition to teaching Q4, I have had the privilege of seeing the fruits of how the Q4 Quest changes lives in a multitude of settings, from personal pastoral counseling to tens-of-thousands of hours of financial planning for families and corporations, as well as vision casting for businesses, non-profit, and even churches.

I owe much of what I've learned through education, life's experiences, and mostly the inheritance of wisdom handed down through selfless relationships and altruistic mentors.

I would like to thank Jeff L, a friend, and mentor, who is a true servant leader and wise beyond his years, who planted this seed many years ago. Jeff has influenced top minds in the financial industry and in business settings across the country, but always found time to always be there for me. I am eternally grateful for his gift to me of asking the right questions with no motive but to empower others. (Always changing lives at the local diner!)

I also want to thank my family for ensuring this project and the life lessons that made it possible beginning with my parents, and especially my dad, who has always been a solid foundation when the storms of life come. Thank you to my two children, Allie and Collin. I thank Allie for teaching me how important our identity truly is. Colin has taught me not to worry about what others think. It wasn't until I came to know the two of you that I understood what unconditional love could be. Thank you to my partner, soul mate, and wife, Alexiea, for whom there are no words to express how blessed I am to have you in my life. I love you all so deeply!

Lastly, I want to thank my Lord and Savior, Jesus Christ. My creator, my rock, my source of life, and my life's purpose. Thank you for life and salvation, for hope and endurance, and mostly for mercy, peace, joy, and love!

WORKS CITED

Nick Leighton, Oct 8, 2019,09:00am EDT, article, Five Reasons Why You Need A Personal Vision Statement (And How To Write One), https://www.forbes.com/sites/forbescoachescouncil/2019/10/08/five-reasons-why-you-need-a-personal-vision-statement-and-how-to-write-one/#3c32acc51ab5

Michael Bazigos and Emily Caruso, March 2, 2016, Article, Why frontline workers are disengaged, https://www.mckinsey.com/business-functions/organization/our-insights/why-frontline-workers-are-disengaged

Rasmus Hougaard, Jacqueline Carter, and Vince Brewerton, January 29, 2018, Article, Why Do So Many Managers Forget They're Human Beings? https://hbr.org/2018/01/why-do-so-many-managers-forget-theyre-human-beings

TESTIMONIES

- "Wow, I am amazed that most of the industry has not figured out what you are teaching here. There is a real need for this..." - David H. (business owner / financial planner)

- "Wow. I will accept all the feedback and guidance you have to offer. I've never really had a program speak to me like yours. You came at a great time as I was just making the promise to myself that I was stepping up to the plate..." - Mike S. R. (rising financial advisor)

- "I feel like my eyes have been opened to a better way and life! Thank you!" - Christina L. (business consultant and advisor)

- "I work with agencies all over the country, and your approach, is truly genius!" - Misty G. (national sales director)

- "I have seen many of the larger firms attempt what we have done together..."- Glenn M. (High-Net-Worth Planning)

- "I continue to learn from you and consider you an extension of my practice and my family. Just thank you!" - Rick F. (financial planner / business owner)

- "Thanks for helping me live the dream!" - Adam G. (retired financial advisor)

www.ingramcontent.com/pod-product-compliance
Lightning Source LLC
Chambersburg PA
CBHW020657220526

45464CB00001B/477